Lifesaving Lessons

Lifesaving Lessons

Notes from an Accidental Mother

Linda Greenlaw

Viking

VIKING
Published by the Penguin Group
Penguin Group (USA) Inc., 375 Hudson Street, New York, New York 10014, U.S.A.
Penguin Group (Canada), 90 Eglinton Avenue East, Suite 700, Toronto, Ontario,
Canada M4P 2Y3 (a division of Pearson Penguin Canada Inc.)
Penguin Books Ltd, 80 Strand, London WC2R 0RL, England
Penguin Ireland, 25 St. Stephen's Green, Dublin 2, Ireland (a division of Penguin Books Ltd)
Penguin Group (Australia), 707 Collins Street, Melbourne,
Victoria 3008 Australia (a division of Pearson Australia Group Pty Ltd)
Penguin Books India Pvt Ltd, 11 Community Centre, Panchsheel Park, New Delhi—110 017, India
Penguin Group (NZ), 67 Apollo Drive, Rosedale, Auckland 0632,
New Zealand (a division of Pearson New Zealand Ltd)
Penguin Books, Rosebank Office Park, 181 Jan Smuts Avenue, Parktown North 2193, South Africa
Penguin China, B7 Jaiming Center, 27 East Third Ring Road North, Chaoyang District, Beijing 100020, China

Penguin Books Ltd, Registered Offices: 80 Strand, London WC2R 0RL, England

First published in 2013 by Viking Penguin,
a member of Penguin Group (USA) Inc.

1 3 5 7 9 10 8 6 4 2

LIBRARY OF CONGRESS CATALOGING-IN-PUBLICATION DATA
Greenlaw, Linda, 1960-
Lifesaving lessons : notes from an accidental mother / Linda Greenlaw.
p. cm.
ISBN 978-0-670-02517-6 (hardback)
1. Greenlaw, Linda, 1960- 2. Foster mothers—Maine—Biography. 3. Foster children—Maine. I. Title.
HQ759.7.G74 2013
306.874—dc23   2012028974

Printed in the United States of America
Set in Adobe Garamond Pro
Designed by Amy Hill

*This book is dedicated to my
wide yet tight group of friends, family,
and community.*

Contents

Lifesaving Lessons

Prologue

Confrontation was imminent. I didn't recall ever fighting with *my* mother the way Mariah and I are now. But I was a different kid. Weird, Mariah would say. The heated arguments she and I were having, I was certain, shook me harder and had more lasting effects on me than they did on the 120-pound fifteen-year-old spitfire who was now quickly closing the gap between us. Mariah seemed to thrive on drama while I cowered from it—it was a mismatched battle at best. When I complained to girlfriends more experienced in the rearing of daughters, they assured me that whatever tiff Mariah and I had gone through was nothing compared to those they had experienced, and that *all* of this was absolutely normal. My girlfriends did not understand.

Maybe if I ignore her, she'll walk right by and leave me in

peace to clean and paint the bottom of the skiff I was now forcing my attention onto. She would never offer to help. That was out of the question. No, I thought, Mariah did not seem to have the gene for motivation. It used to bother me that she could lie on the couch and watch TV while I mowed the lawn, did dishes, or vacuumed the floor around her after I had put in a long day of fishing. But I had come to realize that the wrath of her disposition when asked to pitch in was not worth whatever assistance she rendered. I wondered if that made me an enabler. I squatted behind the upside-down boat—the perfect shield—and scraped tiny barnacles and dried green stuff from the waterline with a wide putty knife. There'll be no ignoring her, I thought as she drew near. She had me in her crosshairs and, it seemed, was trying to press her feet down through the earth with each step. I decided to put her off with a friendly greeting.

Casually looking up from my work, I brushed the blue dust of old antifouling paint from the cuffs of my shirt. I smiled and said, "Hi." Mariah's arms were pumping as wildly as her legs and I could almost feel steam coming from her flared nostrils. I couldn't help but think that she looked like a charging bull. Her brown eyes flashed angrily. Her lips were pursed in a grimace that would repel the meanest junkyard dog, tail between its legs. Wow. I hadn't seen her so mad since I "ruined" her jeans by washing them. (How was I to know that the two-hundred-dollar dungarees were not intended to be laundered in the first six months of wear?) She stopped with the skiff between us, took a deep breath in preparation, and exhaled audibly. Oh yeah, she's pissed, I thought.

"Did you shut off my texting?" The syllables were like bullets fired from an automatic weapon: rapid, and individually articulated to avoid any doubt as to what was asked.

"Yes. First thing this morning," I answered, bracing myself.

"Oh, that is so lame! Why?"

My immediate thought was that my mother would never have tolerated this tone from me. I couldn't imagine that Mariah needed to hear the reasons, yet again, for the no-texting rule. But I knew that if I did not respond quickly, she'd fill the void with total exasperation. "Because you didn't follow the rules. And we can't afford seven-hundred-dollar phone bills every month."

"Your rules are unreasonable. This is totally unfair. And I told you that I would pay the overages." We'd been down this road before. Repeat performance. Bad show. But here we go again, I thought. I went through all the justification I had used the last time I'd received an outrageous bill from the cell phone company, including the fact that I could look on the Internet to see with whom and at what time she was using her phone. Call me old-fashioned, but I think 3,700 text messages a month is excessive. Especially when the text messenger is a full-time student. I expected Mariah to turn her phone off only at the school's required lights-out time, which was 10:00 p.m. I didn't appreciate the 2:00 a.m. text marathons between Mariah and her boyfriend on weeknights. Math had never been my strong suit, but simple subtraction rendered a sum of five hours sleep each night—maximum. Should I mention her poor grades? I wondered.

"It's simple," I said. "You broke the rules. You knew that you'd lose your freedom to text if you couldn't do it responsibly. Besides, how will you go about paying for your overages?"

"I'll use the support checks from my father. You said you wanted nothing to do with that money and that it was mine."

"You're right. I did. Let's see, at this point you are already in arrears for the next five years of support checks. I think those payments terminate on your eighteenth birthday, which is in three years. The numbers don't add up." I could see tears forming in Mariah's eyes. For a tough kid, she sure cried a lot.

"This is stupid!" I cringed at her use of an adjective that had been absolutely forbidden by my own mother. "You *have* to turn it back on. I can't live this way!" Now Mariah was sobbing uncontrollably. Her shoulders shook and her chest heaved. She gasped for a breath and changed tactics, blurting out, "There's nothing to do here. I'm bored!" Ouch, I thought. She knew how I detested her statements of boredom. I always took it so personally. It was as if she were telling me that *I'm* boring. And I am not. Bored? Really, everywhere I looked around my property I saw a project. I was literally surrounded by work. Bored? I'd love to be, even if just for a minute. I wish Mariah could teach me how to be that. No sense rising to that bait, I knew. Nothing good could come from it.

Maybe I didn't have the gene for mothering, but anyone's maternal instincts might naturally get confused by this stage of a child's development. I never knew how to deal with the crying. I wished I didn't see everything in black and white. I wished I could react with more compassion. If Mariah were younger, I'd probably hug her and stroke her hair until she stopped. I had no desire to hug her now. And she had no desire to be hugged.

There was an awkward silence, except for the sniffling. Weary and fearing going another round, I secretly wished Mariah would spin abruptly on her heel and stomp off as she always did. Why doesn't she sulk back to the house and watch *Gossip Girl* and read *Cosmopolitan* magazine? I picked up the masking tape and began to stretch it along the line where the skiff's blue and gray paint met. "You can't simply dismiss me like that! I am not a member of your crew!"

Well, that's for sure, I thought as I kept taping without looking up. "No member of my crew would ever talk to me like that."

"Please turn my texting back on." Now the tears had dried and Mariah's tone had changed from fighting to pleading. "I'll follow the rules this time. I promise."

"No. I'm sorry. Last month was your third and final last chance. Your texting is off until I see your grades. And then, if we can have a civil discussion and come to some agreement about use, I may give you one more shot."

"You cannot be serious! This is so stupid!" Mariah's face was getting red again. Here comes the next flood of tears, I thought. Her eyes darted wildly back and forth between me and the house. Oh, take the house, I thought. Please take the house. I knew from past experience that Mariah would eventually retreat and she'd miraculously be wearing a smile by lunchtime. But this time her departure would not be without a parting shot. In total frustration, she grabbed a quart of paint, then turned and hurled it into the woods so far that I wondered if I'd ever find it. "You are not my mother! I want to go home!"

CHAPTER I

An Island Life for Me

Of course Mariah was right. I was not her mother. I had never had any children. I was the somewhat notoriously single and childless Linda Greenlaw. Although I am living what in my mind is a charmed life, even as I was cruising through my forties, I didn't have time for kids, or a husband for that matter. My childbearing and rearing years had been spent fully immersed in my life's work and greatest passion. They were spent at sea, chasing swordfish.

I never imagined that I would end up alone and childless. In fact, in my earlier years, I had always taken for granted that I would eventually re-create what *I* had had growing up: a loving, traditional family complete with hubby and kiddos. But things didn't quite work out that way. Consumed by, and in love with, the excitement and adventure and challenge of the life and lifestyle of commercial fishing since the age of nineteen, I always felt fulfilled in a way that might have upstaged the quest for mate and babies. I guess I thought I always had plenty of time for family. Middle age had sneaked up behind me while I was looking over the bow.

When I'm not offshore, I reside on Isle au Haut, a tiny island, with an even tinier population, off the coast of Maine. My life on the island is as salty as my life offshore in that I spend my time fishing for lobster, halibut, herring, or digging for clams, basically harvesting anything that swims or crawls around the shores surrounding my home. Of course I also write about these things, leaving me with a fairly short résumé: I fish, offshore and on, and I write about fishing. Writing is as solitary and antisocial as fishing. The solitude and remoteness of island existence and life at sea are conducive to prolific writing and are sources of material and stimulation. But those same attributes have stunted my personal relationships. The years I spent at sea, mostly thirty days at a time, didn't do much for my love life either. There's just something about "Thanks for dinner. See you in a month" that doesn't lead to a second date. All of this amounts to what I would call "family nonplanning." Living on a remote outpost with tenuous ties (weather permitting) to mainline mainland hasn't done any more for the prospect of having my own family than my life at sea has. I didn't plan it that way. That's just the way it is. Ask anyone. They'll tell you that I am the woman who survived "the perfect storm." And not only did I survive that devastating and life-taking weather event of 1991, but I also managed through my undying pragmatism to make the most of it. I have published, let's see, eight books, taking advantage of the spotlight Sebastian Junger put on me when he called me "one of the best captains, period, on the entire East Coast." And the readers of my more memoirlike work will attest to the fact that I do not have children. When I lamented my single and childless status in *The Lobster Chronicles,* my older sister jokingly referred to the book as a 260-page personal ad. And as my status has not changed, I have to consider the possibility that it wasn't well written. I hear my fellow islanders whispering "old maid" comments that no longer embarrass me, so I guess I have progressed beyond that particular sensitivity. For that reason, when Mariah reminded me, in the heat of battle, that I was not her mother, I suppose an appropriate response aimed at her level would have been, "Duh." But for your edification, let me explain how Mariah came to be on my cell phone bill in the first place. It all began on that same tiny island, just a few years ago.

The new guy hadn't been on the island long before the residents had all formed strong opinions. When you quite literally reside on a rock, seven miles from the mainland, with fewer than fifty other humans in the off-season, you get to know more about your neighbors than those who dwell in tamer, more populated areas. However, the trend toward more newcomers to the island leveled off when they didn't winter well. Most of them bailed out following their first icy, lonely season, and just when the rest of us were beginning to warm to them. Because of this, I hadn't had much to do with the new guy directly; it seemed like wasting time if he was going to leave anyway. My opinion of Ken Howard was based primarily on what friends and neighbors who had taken time to get to know him a bit had told me. They'd said he was a decent guy. Moving to Isle au Haut from Memphis, Tennessee, had been Ken's lifelong dream, and now, in his midforties, he was going for it. He had visited the island as a boy with his grandparents, and that visit had left such a profound impression that he spent nearly thirty years working to fulfill his dream. I had to respect that. And he had with him his ten-year-old niece, named Mariah. Ken, the story goes, had saved his niece from an existence of poverty, drugs, abuse, et cetera, bringing her to what he remembered as a paradise so that she, too, could have a dream to pursue. And with our island's one-room schoolhouse at its lowest attendance in years, anyone with a kid was welcomed with open arms. And hey, let's face it, the addition of an eligible bachelor who was no one's blood relative, was ambulatory, and could drive after dark was intriguing to some of us.

Three years into his being here, my firsthand interactions with Ken Howard hadn't gone beyond "Hi. Nice day." I had learned that he was a recovering alcoholic, and he appeared to be sober when we had chance encounters. Ken had successfully weathered three tough winters, but one prevalent theory about new people who *do* stay is that they are misfits who can't survive in mainstream, orthodox civilization. And who wants to hang with weirdos? So between residents' not wanting to waste time on someone whom the odds are against staying long enough to get to know well enough to truly dislike, and the idea that anyone who does stay is a social oddball, new people have a tough row to hoe. I have a bumper sticker on my truck that reads, "Some of us are here because we're not all there." So when Ken pulled into the end of my driveway one summer morning about two years after he moved to the island, I was perplexed. He climbed out of his VW Rabbit and I continued to focus on the pot warp I was measuring, cutting, and splicing while he strongly urged his niece to get out of the car. In all honesty, I couldn't recall seeing Mariah out of the vehicle since her arrival on Isle au Haut, unless it was in front of the school sitting on a swing, not swinging, just sitting. Because there are only thirteen miles of road on our island, and the price of gasoline is exorbitant, I supposed that if you like being in a car, you'll spend an inordinate amount of time just sitting in park. Whether it was the store parking lot or the area beside the Town Hall, Mariah seemed most content within the car, looking out. Well, we all thought, she was thirteen—and seemed perfectly thirteen in her nonamusement and disinterest in everyone and everything around her.

Now, as Ken cajoled Mariah to get out of the Rabbit, I pretended not to notice them out of politeness that could have easily been misconstrued as rudeness. After Ken pulled Mariah from her safe haven, I looked up from my work and called the usual greeting, which was met with a relieved smile and half wave from Ken and a frightened stare from the girl who appeared to be making a concerted effort to move slowly enough to remain behind her uncle.

Ken stomped out a cigarette in the dirt and waited for the young girl to catch up before speaking. "Mariah needs some work, and I was wondering if you had anything." His voice was deep and sexy, and not at all compatible with the very thin man whose hair was too long and could have stood a good washing. I thought he looked better when he had first arrived on island. But sometimes Isle au Haut has that effect on people. Most of us get very casual about personal appearance. There's an overwhelming aura of "Who's going to see me anyway?" And "needs" seemed ill fitting when used in reference to employment for this waif of a preteen kid. "Do you need a sternman?" Ken continued. I held back a chuckle. "She's available tomorrow and every day until school starts up in the fall. She's a really hard worker. You're a great role model for her, Linda." Although Ken's lack of a Maine accent clearly marked him as one "from away," the black-and-red-plaid hunting shirt and missing front tooth placed him in good stead.

I had intended to fish my lobster traps alone this season, concentrating more on a newly acquired herring-seining business. But I did plan to hire someone to paint buoys and do a few odd jobs. "Do you want a job?" I asked, looking at Mariah directly for maybe the first time ever.

There was a short pause while I waited for Mariah to reply. Ken wasn't patient, and I supposed that came from knowing the girl as only a close relative could. I suspected that he feared what Mariah might say. "She does. She really does. And she's a great little worker. I just want to teach her the value of hard work and being productive. She hasn't had much of that in her past." That seemed noble enough, I thought. I repeated my question.

I stared at Mariah, whose face was getting quite red, unsure whether the increased color was anger or total humiliation. She still hadn't opened her mouth, but she finally had to make eye contact. I shrugged and waited. Ken took a step to the side, eliminating the bit of protection she had. She took a deep breath, as if bracing herself for some trauma, exhaled loudly and said, "I guess." I took that as a yes, and had a fleeting notion that the attitude might be an issue.

Never one to back away from a challenge, I said, "You can start painting buoys tomorrow. The paint and brushes are in the front of my truck." I proceeded to show Mariah where to hang the wet buoys to dry, and told her that we'd begin setting lobster traps as soon as she had enough buoys ready. My new sternman looked as horrified as any indentured servant who suddenly realizes there is no escape.

"Thanks, Linda. She'll be here tomorrow morning, first thing. You won't be disappointed," Ken said as he pulled a fresh pack of Marlboros from his shirt pocket. "Thank Linda, Mariah," he advised the thoroughly disgusted girl.

"Thanks." It was the longest, most exaggerated *Th* sound in history. She couldn't have been less sincere. It seemed that working for me might have been punishment for something. I had no idea what she had done to warrant what she clearly saw as torture. But I surely knew the value of hard work, and believed that the insolent teen might benefit from some. I hadn't seemed like much of a prospect as a commercial swordfisherman when I landed my first job on the deck of a boat—or "site," as we say—at the age of nineteen. Someone had given me a chance, and that had become my life's work and first love. And I despise painting buoys.

And so our relationship was born. It became abundantly clear that the only things that suited Mariah about working for me were the schedule and the paycheck. If I were to use a metaphor of my time being a writing project, I'd say that the bulk of the pages produced in early spring had been working on a new fishing venture: leaving lobster fishing small doodle space in the margins of life. I had acquired a herring-seining operation from my best friend, Alden, and had hoped to cash in on catching and selling herring to fellow lobster fishermen to use as bait. Spring is notoriously poor for lobster fishing, and it always appears that the only people making money are those selling bait. As a result, I never entered the margins to set or tend my traps until 10:00 a.m., which suited my new helper just fine. Most full-time, 800-trap fishermen work every day starting before the sun comes up until it sets, but our fishing duty was fairly light. I didn't set all my traps. We fished only 300, and hauled just four short days each week, hauling 150 traps each time we went out. Coupled with the fact that I had to spend some time writing, I *dabbled* in lobster fishing in comparison to the full-time guys whose only income comes from what they pull out of a trap.

I think it is fair to say that Mariah hated every second spent aboard my lobster boat, *Mattie Belle*. She hated the bait, handling the lobsters, picking crabs from traps, cleaning the boat, and she suffered from seasickness. That is not to say she wasn't good at all of it. In fact, she learned the moves quickly, and was one of the best helpers I ever hired. I never told her how to do anything. She watched me do something once, then dove in and took over. She watched how I used my legs to throw a trap high onto a stack, and did the same. She watched how I pulled a trap up onto the rail of the boat, clearing the line through the block, and mimicked me, pulling every other trap aboard. We seldom spoke. I do recall her saying on her first day, after throwing up for the first

time, "I'll never like this." And I still recall my reply being something to the effect that she would learn to love it. We didn't speak
another word the rest of the day. She didn't have to say a word to
communicate clearly to me that she found the entire experience
excruciating. The whole summer long, Mariah would show up at
the dock at the very minute required, not one second early or late.
It was remarkable. Anyone could have set their watch by her bicycle's coasting down the hill leading to the float where I was
always waiting for her in the skiff. The daily skiff ride to the
mooring was perhaps the only time Mariah ever smiled during
the course of the season. She would perch on the bow, face forward, and let the wind blow her thick, blond hair back straight,
looking quite like the bowsprit Kate Winslet aboard the *Titanic*
until we stopped alongside of the *Mattie Belle*. Her hair would
fall, she would quickly gather it into a neat ponytail, exhale audibly in expectation of yet another day of misery, climb out of
the skiff, and board the boat. She had her own boots and wore a
set of my oilskins, not the highest fashion for a girl of her age who
hadn't lazed into the island's casual sloppiness yet.

As the season wore on, Mariah and I did talk. Mostly it was
my initiative. I understood that we had little in common and
didn't want to be her friend. But I did become quite fond of her
tenacity and tolerant of her poor attitude. I took seriously my part
in role modeling. Mariah spent time with other island women,
which was great as we all knew that her uncle could be everything
except female. And every young girl needs to have adult women
in her life, and without a mother around, the island women filled
in expertly. Most of the mothering was done by my good friend

and neighbor Brenda, which seemed entirely appropriate to me. Brenda looks and, well, just *is* more motherly than I am in that she engages in more feminine activities than I do and has raised both a daughter and a son. Before moving to the island from the Camden area, Brenda worked as a hair stylist and in a bank. Brenda is always neat as a pin in her personal appearance, even when she is helping her husband, Bill, in the stern of his boat, or collecting the island's trash to fulfill the contract they have with the town to do so. Brenda is also the island's librarian. Call me a sexist, but the stereotypical librarian is female, right? Whereas I was the adult tomboy still in fishing gear, Brenda was far from the dowdy stereotype. She's stylish to the point where I have always marveled at the perfection of her fingernails knowing that she picks crabmeat all summer. Come to think of it, Bill was a wonderful father figure for Mariah in that he shares good advice with those he sees in need (and in my opinion he is always spot on). Bill and Brenda each have families of their own from previous marriages, including several children and a couple of grandkids. Divorced, newly married, and fully established on Isle au Haut, they had all the experience I might have lacked in parenting. Mariah would go to Bill and Brenda's on a regular basis and bake cookies or do crafts or whatever girl things were occurring at the time. Mariah became close to Bill and Brenda, even calling them Grammy and Grampy, though they're not that much older than me. Isle au Haut has always been the epitome of how it takes a village to raise a child, even if there are only a handful of them on the island. And Mariah benefited from that in a big way.

Mariah was a serious kid who rarely laughed. I imagine this was due mostly to the seasickness. The only fun she seemed to have with me that season was when we retaliated for some light-hearted teasing she endured at the hands of a couple of island fishermen who enjoyed taunting her on the radio when they knew Mariah could hear them and they could see her. She had been tagged with the nickname "Pork Chop." She detested the name— what weight-conscious adolescent girl wouldn't?—but liked the attention of the men well enough. When they spoke of a "Pork Chop sighting in Moore's Harbor," she'd throw her hands in the air and stomp her feet, much to the delight of the men who watched her antics and then commented, bringing on the next flailing of arms and stomping. It became a ritual on our fishing days. I promised Mariah we would get back at them before the end of the season, and we did.

One day, after having been off island for a shopping trip the day before, Mariah coasted down to the dock with a rubber pork chop she'd bought at a pet store. As we hauled traps that day we saved the garbage that comes up in them that is usually discarded. On our way back to the mooring, we sneakily hauled a trap belonging to the biggest instigator of the teasing and stuffed it full of sea cucumbers, sea urchins, crabs, seaweed, even a broken pump that we found aboard the *Mattie Belle*. When we couldn't fit another piece of bycatch into the trap, we topped it with the plastic pork chop that Mariah had placed in the man's bait bag. We forced the trap closed, and it took both of us pushing as hard as we could to get it back overboard. The trap splashed, and Mariah had a look of satisfaction as she cleaned the

Mattie Belle all the way to the mooring. The sabotaged trap was directly in front of my house, so I was able to watch it being hauled and give Mariah a play-by-play account over the phone. It was great—we were both laughing hysterically. And that was the one and only time I heard Mariah laugh all summer.

And it was, I thought, a shame that Mariah wasn't more of a happy-go-lucky sort. There were times when I wanted to take her by the shoulders and shake her, and tell her to look around. It was summer! All the other island kids were elated at that time of year, along with everyone else. Summer is idyllic on our island. Summers on Isle au Haut are like those you read about: romantic and fantastic. The year-rounders are out of hibernation with the exuberance of daffodils proudly pushing through newly thawed ground as if sprung from tight coils. The youngest kids, year-round and seasonal alike, scramble from tidal pool to tidal pool, delighted with shelled treasures and undaunted by wet sneakers. The time line of growing painlessly is measured from those tidal pools and periwinkles to outboard motors and mackerel. For children the island is a paradise where their safety is checked at the high-water mark with life jackets worn below and helmets above. It's a free and special existence where parents worry only about bruises and barnacle scrapes in a place that harbors no other threats to children.

Not just a paradise for kids, the island has the ability to bring out the kid in all of us. Sun-filled days end with colorful sunsets crowned by starry nights, eliciting contented sighs accompanied by goose bumps that rise in answer to the breeze cooled by its travel across Penobscot Bay. Vacationers are somehow lighter in the absence of cell phones (which rarely work here) and e-mail and responsibility. The Island Store (the only grocery game in town) is bursting at the seams all summer long with people and conversation and laughter. The absolute hub of activity, the store is quirky in its shelving of goods (baked beans next to the duck confit). An island that isn't high on regulations or standards knows nothing of exceeding legal or even practical occupancy. This is obvious not only in the store but also at Sunday service in the only church, potluck dinners at the Town Hall, dances with "island music," or the annual pie auction where people are ridiculously happy to pay three hundred dollars for whatever Pat Marks has concocted with peaches to pay for whatever the schoolteacher has in mind for the next field trip. Seemingly responsible adults are enthusiastically and unapologetically childish in summer. Even so, the kids always come first.

The entire island took interest in each and every kid's well-being. While I had always been aware of this characteristic, it grew stronger with each day that passed while Mariah and I fished together. Friends and neighbors thanked me for giving her the opportunity to spend time with me. I thought it was odd that people would actually thank me for doing such an obviously right thing (however reluctantly I had done it). But I did appreciate the sentiment, and her uncle had been right—she was indeed a great worker. Even the summer people took notice of the beautiful young girl who seemed to be blossoming and flourishing before their eyes. I took it upon myself to urge Mariah to apply to a private boarding school on the mainland. She did, and was accepted and granted full scholarship money. The island school only goes through the eighth grade, and the option other than a boarding school is the forty-minute boat ride and twenty-minute bus trip back and forth every day to attend the closest public high school—not a good schedule for a girl who clearly craved a bit of extracurricular life. We started to think of other ways to help out. A friend split the cost of a much needed orthodontist, and Mariah was soon in full braces. When it came time for new school clothes, summer people pitched in generously. "Our" little girl was thriving and we all took great pride in sending her off to school. Nobody was prouder than Ken. He paced nervously back and forth across the deck of the mail boat while the entire island community wished Mariah well and prepared to wave good-bye to the beaming girl in the stern of the boat.

Some of us had even shed tears as we watched her step aboard the mail boat with suitcase and uncle, not to return to what had certainly become her home until Thanksgiving. When it was my turn for a hug, she had whispered, "You lied to me." I backed up to arm's length. "I never grew to love it."

"You'll beg me for your job back next summer," I said smiling.

"Not a chance."

CHAPTER 2

Restless Waters

There is a certain look in a person's eyes when he or she says something that will never be retracted. "Never say never" is well and good, but there are exceptions. And I knew without a doubt that Mariah would *never* work in the stern of the *Mattie Belle* with me again. She had, I supposed, learned enough about the meaning of hard work to know that she wanted no part of it. That is as valuable a lesson as any for a young girl headed off to school. She was now armed with the knowledge that she did not want to be like so many island kids who know hard work to the exclusion of higher education. For some, fishing is their life's work, and love. For others, it is a rut they fall into that family ties keep them from ever climbing out of. And yet here I am, someone most people consider an anomaly—educated, and still working like an idiot, much to my nonfishing family's dismay.

All in all, I felt good bidding Mariah farewell, as I knew I had at least provided her with a real-life example of gender being a nonissue as well as the merits of finding work you can love. I do like what I do. Well, most of the time. I was in the midst of making a few changes in my life—both personally and professionally— mostly in the spirit of remaining a rolling stone. (So much for the notion of settling down.) I deeply regretted not figuring out that I wanted no part of moss gathering in the decade that I'd tried it. But that's me for you. Ten years seemed like a real mark, a decade in which a line graph would indicate a straight line, marked on either end by acute angles. I had changed my life quite dramatically ten years before when I moved to the rock longing for the stability of family from the more fluid, nearly twenty years of blue water fishing. In the period of living and breathing salt water and swordfish, I had always been accused of being irresponsible because all I owned fit nicely into a garbage bag that was easily flung from back of truck to deck of boat while my contemporaries practiced capitalism and consumerism. In the decade that I tried to fit in, accumulating all the requisite household bills and chores, I had a long-standing (if mostly long-distance) relationship with a really good guy, Simon; had built a house; and bought my own boat and fishing gear. Mortgaged to the hilt, and seemingly settled down with a nice guy, I learned that responsibility didn't hold a candle to what I had given up to try it out. Now, at the far end of the decade, I once again longed for real change, change that looked more like total irresponsibility. I knew the impetus for change was the calendar. A decade had been long enough. A decade had been ample time for Simon to propose marriage, which he had chosen to not do. We shared a fun, healthy relationship. But I wanted more. Simon is more of the "If it ain't broke, don't fix it" type. So had I wasted ten years? Wasted seemed too harsh, I thought. But I sure wish it hadn't taken so long to eliminate Simon as a possibility. Yup, my future would look different.

I would be fishing even fewer lobster traps in the future. I certainly would not have enough work to employ anyone in that business even if Mariah did an about-face and wanted to go. I had recently been purposefully navigating toward a future less about lobster and more toward other things. I would write and promote my books, get my herring-seining business up and running, and spend the fall at sea in the blue water chasing swordfish. I figured that Mariah, in time, would steer her future in some direction, and I'd hear about that through the usual island chain of communication when it happened. But for now, she had four years of high school to complete before the next big decision. She would be guided by her uncle, her guidance counselors and advisers at school, and of course her huge island family.

The island kids were all back in school—some away and some staying close to home. The summer residents all trickled off the island—those with schoolkids leaving as early as August, and retirees hanging on until Columbus Day weekend. I got third-hand reports of Mariah's exploits at boarding school, all of which sounded absolutely normal. She was back on the island for Thanksgiving and Christmas. I ran into her both times briefly, exchanged hugs, and offered work, the latter of which she politely refused. From our short conversations, I gathered that she hadn't found her niche yet at school. She didn't have anything she was very enthusiastic about (unless boys count). I understand that endless questions of a fifteen-year-old high school freshman from so many caring adults must certainly be tedious at best, so Mariah's lack of animation was not surprising, seeing as I was likely the umpteenth person to quiz her. I continued in our few chance encounters to be upbeat about work—still being as good a role model as I could. Not that she noticed.

It wasn't until midwinter that I also fell into a slight funk and once again pondered whether I was on the right path. Most people my age were settled and staid, and change was the last thing on their minds. Although it may seem strange to some that I would question my what and why while gaining on the half-century mark, it may in part be a tendency that goes along with being single and childless. Think about it: I had nobody else to consider. I had too much time to dwell on myself. Teenagers do not corner that market! With Mariah long out of sight and mind, the role model was put to bed, and I was able to fully indulge in selfishness without worrying who might be influenced by my negativity. I remember well my low point.

One midwinter morning, on the shore not far from my parents' house, I found myself in quite a predicament. The float on which I had stored all my herring gear had broken free of its mooring in a storm and had been left high and dry on the rocks. Crawling on hands and knees under the float over the seaweed-covered ledges, I crouched to avoid the beam I'd found earlier. I slowly made my way to the last elliptical piece of daylight that streamed through the gap between two of the newly secured pieces of Styrofoam I had pilfered from a float even more derelict than the one I was now under and trying so hard to resurrect. Come to think of it, I had more or less borrowed without permission this entire raft onto which my herring crew and I had hastily bailed nearly four hundred fathoms of seine gear last fall. I had been in a hurry to wrap up the business of catching herring for lobster bait (or not catching, as it turned out) to jump aboard a sword boat and head east for a quick trip. I'd declared the abandoned float on the beach next to the town landing "mine," launched it, piled it full of twine, and secured it to a summer person's mooring. Now I was paying for my haste. And now it was February. The float full of my investment had chaffed its bridle and swum with wind and current under the cover of darkness right out of the thoroughfare and onto the rocky shore below the Dices' summer cottage where the tide had left it high and dry four nights ago.

Barnacles had taken their toll on my hands. Thin, crooked lines of blood were much like reflections of the crow's-feet at the corners of my eyes that were most noticeable at 5:30 that morning when I'd rushed by the bathroom mirror in a yank to reach the shore while the tide was out. My hands were too cold to feel the sting. I imagine I looked somewhat seallike, slithering on the slippery ledges out from beneath the float on my belly. The tiniest snowflakes drifted in on the northwest breeze, adding a note of chill to the already frigid scene. A distinct, white stripe of frozen salt water ringed the shore at the high-water mark, and lily pad ice dallied on the surface of the cove north of us. The "us" I refer to wasn't the group I would have expected. My herring crew, or Omega Four, as we had named ourselves last spring when we were all so proud and excited to launch the new business, were now as scattered as the fish had been all season. Dave Hiltz and Bill Clark and his son Nate were nowhere to be found. The "us" present here now and assisting with labor and advice in this potential disaster consisted of perhaps the most unlikely group of guys to band together, even in the face of adversity. But that's the island way. Bad things happen. The results are sometimes good. Good and bad actions and what lies in their wake do a dance of fleeting and lingering here on the island. Grudges are held dear and hatchets are seldom buried. That said, there's an overlying sentiment of "love the one you're with."

And those whom I was with right now included Howard Blatchford, fellow island fisherman, and Simon and his son Todd, who had come from their permanent homes in Vermont for a winter weekend of torching burn piles they had stacked up in the drier, unsafe burning months. Simon is the guy with whom I had been in a more or less romantic relationship over the last eight years. Little did father and son (retired orthopedic surgeon and brand-new dermatologist) know that they would end up helping me with the disaster that had been left by a particularly high tide. Whether Simon and Todd had come to offer assistance out of loyalty or pity, I wasn't sure. My uncertainty about my future with Simon was on my mind, but my current time of need was hardly the moment to sever my relationship with him, I reasoned with myself.

Howard extended a calloused hand to help me to my feet. I stretched out straight, both hands on my lower back, and groaned a little. "I don't know what more we can do. That's all the Styrofoam," I said to the three men who shifted uneasily on weed-covered rocks and looked as cold as I felt. "I'll wait for the tide to come in and see if she floats."

"It went ashore on a nine-point-six tide, and this afternoon is just a nine-footer," Howard said softly, almost apologetically, as if he were embarrassed to have to tell me what the tide was doing. "Friday morning, eight-thirty. We'll have eleven feet. The moon, well, you know." He diverted his eyes to the toes of his boots as his voice trailed off. The fact that he had a graying, kinked ponytail protruding from beneath his wool watch cap bothered me. I don't know why.

"I hope it doesn't take until Friday. I'm worried sick that this rickety, old float will break apart and leave the Dices with a lawn ornament," I said, nearly praying and not mentioning my financial investment that would be a total loss if the raft collapsed or was beaten to pieces in the surf should a storm come along. I also had in mind the monumental sweat equity of the other 75 percent of Omega Four when I decided to remain on the beach and keep a fretful watch while the three men who had been here to help left to do other things, promising to return at high tide. Simon and Todd's presence, and help, made me feel even gloomier as it amplified the fact that I had no such relationship of my own, and that I had been in this seemingly go-nowhere romance forever, and now felt that I was using Simon. I had, I reasoned, agreed to feed the men all weekend. But somehow "Will work for food" not being on the doctors' agendas made me feel a little sleazy. As already stated, my disposition was unusually down, allowing me to wallow in selfish thoughts of how desperate my situation was both personally and professionally in the immediate predicament in spite of the fact that if I had examined my life at all, I would have noticed that I had little to complain about. So I would focus on how the float teetering on the brink of disaster might be a microcosm for my life in general. When friends had voiced similar complaints, I hadn't had much patience and always advised that they change something. "You are solely responsible for your own happiness" was something I needn't hear now in echo.

Two trucks started on the hill behind me—Simon and Todd in one, and Howard in the other. I never turned to wave good-bye or to thank them, but instead stood staring at the incoming tide as it teasingly lapped the lower corner of the stranded float. As soon as the noise of the trucks had dissipated to a distance that I knew would prohibit the men from seeing me, I made my way to a perfect and natural seat in the ledges and sat sheltered from the nipping breeze. Soon the sun poked through the clouds still spitting light snow and lent enough warmth to penetrate the layers of oilskins, sweater, and wool shirt I had carefully chosen this morning knowing that I had a long day ahead of me. Waiting for the tide to rise or fall, which is something islanders spend a lot of time doing, is much like watching the proverbial pot that never boils. But today I didn't mind this seemingly do-nothing time as I managed to convince myself that I was actually engaged in the activity of figuring things out. Not that I expected any real revelations in the next two hours. But the truth was, I hadn't taken much time to just sit and think lately—about the stuck float and about a lot of other things in my life that seemed to be stuck, too.

My first thoughts were about the actual situation at hand. What if Howard was right, and the tide wouldn't rise to a height that would float my gear off these ledges until Friday? This was only Sunday. What were the chances of the float's holding together through five more days and nights of rising and falling and surging up and down, on and off this unforgiving, rocky shore? The ledges in this particular area were steep and jagged. The float had landed on a sharp, peaked ledge that was now gnawing through a major cross member that if broken would be the end of any hope of recovering my seine gear. When the raft half floated, it looked good. When it was hard aground, it appeared to be bent in the middle and threatening to snap in two. A tiny voice deep in my mind whispered, "That might be a blessing in disguise." Stifling the voice, I went back to figuring a way out of this, short of giving up and letting nature run its course, which is how my gear ended up here in the first place. Or, at least, that was the story I was buying as opposed to the conspiracy theory that rumbled through the island's rumor mill. Winter is rough out here, I knew. But who would be bored or hateful enough to sabotage me?

Even at high tide there wasn't enough depth of water to pull a boat alongside the offshore edge of the float in an attempt to rescue the netting or twine from it. The twine itself—I couldn't venture a guess at how much it weighed. Four hundred fathoms long, ten fathoms deep, with a leaded line on the bottom edge and corks to float the top edge, allowing the net to hang vertically in the water like a fence—just the twenty-four thousand square feet of webbing was enough to squat the float low into the water prior to hitting the beach. Half of my gear was configured into a purse seine, which has big brass rings along the bottom through which a rope or purse line runs that can be cinched to gather the bottom of the net together to capture whatever fish are encircled. The purse also sports extra-heavy mesh on the bunting end to reinforce the twine when a great weight of fish is lifted through the water. It was quite a mountain of gear, for sure. And right now the inexperienced eye might describe it as a mess. But it was actually quite organized with the end of the top piece of twine clearly marked for ease of loading into dories (double-ended, nonpowered boats designed to carry fishing gear). If the float broke apart, there would be no ease of anything. I hoped the extra Styrofoam flotation we had just spent hours securing under and all around the bottom lip of the deck would add enough buoyancy to the raft to allow it to be pulled off the rocks. At this point, scuttling the whole works would be more of an embarrassment than any significant loss. But I had to admit that this herring adventure, not unlike many of my bright, salty ideas, had been a bust. Just because you call yourself a fisherman doesn't mean you catch fish. Not a natural at anything, like everything else in my experience, I had a fairly flat learning curve for herring seining.

The sun was out in force now. Its beam on the water stung my eyes. So I closed them and easily drifted back to the warm and not so distant memory of great anticipation of slamming the herring. My crew—Dave Hiltz, Bill Clark, his son Nate—and I spent a very ambitious day and a half early last spring, driven by visions of dollar signs, working like mules to get the bottoms of three dories scraped and painted and launched, and six hundred fathoms of herring twine aboard Alden's boat, the *Grace Egretta*. The dories that we literally slapped antifouling paint on were the best of the bunch strewn around Alden's shorefront on Orr's Island, and were part of a package I agreed to, sight unseen. The guys and I had driven my Jeep to Alden's place with a plan to return home via water with our new herring venture in tow. Things went pretty much according to plan. Alden had seine twine in heaps all over the place—some on the wharf, some under tarps above the shore, and some stored in and on top of old truck bodies. Somewhat disorganized, Alden did manage to show us where things were and even dug up a couple of old paintbrushes from his fish house, or "condo," as he delights in calling it. Although he kept assuring me that I was buying the best of what he had, when some of the twine ripped when pulled between two fingers, I had my doubts. It was too late to back out now. We had already named our business and had calculated the money we'd all save by catching our own bait and the profits we'd realize by selling what we couldn't use ourselves—and all cash to boot! I have never said, and never will say, that Alden ripped me off. I know he believes (mistakenly) that I got the better end of the bargain. "Do you know what it would cost to have a dory that size built today?"

"You mean as opposed to the year 1920, when it *was* built?" After a few of these friendly yet pointed exchanges, I let it go. What the hell, if Alden had fished this crap and made money, I guessed we could, too. Besides, it was his boat, *Grace Egretta,* that I wanted. And I was soon at her helm, bringing her alongside Alden's wharf to load the twine. Named for his mother, *Grace*

Egretta was every bit as classy and stalwart. One of the more recently constructed wooden boats in the retro phase on the coast of Maine, she was bigger and much more capable than my own lobster boat, the *Mattie Belle*. The real advantage was the mast and boom she was equipped with and the hydraulic-powered purse block that is used to haul the twine, allowing my crew and me to step right into the present century rather than live in the past and basically manhandle miles of seine twine. Of course the first rule of business—especially business with pals—is to set it all down in writing. I should have spelled out my expectations to Alden, and he should have done the same with me. I believed I had given him a down payment on the boat. He believed I had purchased his junky herring gear and was borrowing the boat for delivery purposes only. Even if possession is indeed nine-tenths of the law, when it's Alden on the last tenth, you may as well give it up. But that didn't come until later.

So on this bright summer day (in my dream reverie), with a mountainous thirty-six thousand square feet of net filling the cockpit, and towing three dories single file behind us, we left Lowell's Cove and struck a course for home looking like a mother duck leading her triplets. Alden stood in his skiff and drifted by the mooring we had just dropped and waved until we couldn't see him anymore. He sure looked sad.

It was an ideal day for towing dories the eight-hour steam between Orr's Island and Isle au Haut, and I wasn't long forgetting Alden's forlorn good-bye and thinking ahead to happier things, like making money. Oh sure, we had plenty of work to do before we could actually catch fish. But we were all fairly gung ho and excited about engaging in a fishery different from the lobstering that hadn't been overly productive due to low prices and high expenses (one of which was bait, and we had a remedy for that now). Nate stretched out on the top of the twine, and Dave claimed a bunk down forward in the cabin while Bill and I sat in the wheelhouse and made a list of things to do before we could make proper use of our new acquisition.

Our arrival that afternoon into a glistening Penobscot Bay was special. We were filled with all the hope and goodwill that any bunch of friends embarking on an adventure would be. The first leg of the journey was complete. The dories were anchored in the thoroughfare at the town float where we could begin fixing their rails and refastening their guts. One dory needed a new stern fiberglassed into her as she appeared to have a big bite taken out of that end where the twine would catch when sliding from within to overboard during the setting process. All three dories needed some work before we could fill them with the seine gear they are designed to carry. I breathed a sigh of relief when we put the *Grace Egretta* on a mooring right in front of my house. I thought I'd feel pretty good looking at her first thing each morning. We went ashore by way of the town dock and were greeted with the fanfare appropriate for fishermen returning home with something that resembled employment and, more important, a way to provide bait to islanders, saving them the steam to the mainland that they would otherwise make. A few of the crustier guys shook their heads at the condition of our dories. But we had half expected it as that, too, is an island thing—negativity—especially when someone else is doing something constructive.

The head shakers and naysayers got fairly quiet in the days that followed when they saw how absolutely driven we were and how nice the first two dories came out. Bill, Nate, and Dave all neglected their lobster businesses to go hard at the herring venture. As soon as the first dory was repaired, we filled it with the first two hundred fathoms of running twine from the top of the pile aboard the *Grace Egretta,* mending holes and tears as we went. The holes and tears were quite numerous and it became obvious that Alden had a unique way of keeping his gear fishable. He hadn't, as far as I could tell, ever actually mended a hole in the net. He "puckered" holes and "laced" the straight cuts or tears. Puckering is where the twine around a hole is pulled together and tied in an overhand knot. It's "gommie," a Maine word that means sloppy or untidy. Something done quickly and roughly is said to be gommed together, but quicker than "slugging," or patching, with a new piece of netting to fill the hole. Lacing is similar to how a shoelace works. A piece of mending twine (like string) loaded on a special tool called a twine needle is pulled through the meshes on either side of a torn area; the mending twine is dispensed from the needle; and when a bit of tension is applied, it acts to draw the sides of the tear together, eliminating the places where fish can escape. We had no new twine with which to slug, so we got good at puckering and lacing. Some pieces of the net were so fragile from rot, they tore even more in the process of mending. Meshes popped from even the gentlest tug with the twine needle. It was frustrating, but we eventually had two dories full of some fairly tender "running twine."

The running twine, as opposed to the purse seine, is used to shut off a cove or piece of shoreline after fish arrive there. One end of the seine is run ashore and tied to a tree or some other solid object. Once the end is secure, the dory carrying the bulk of the net is towed behind a boat around the targeted body of fish while the net spills into the water over the stern of the dory. The other end of the seine is also made fast to the shore so that the school of fish is surrounded or shut off from any exit. (Hence the importance of having no gaping holes.) Once the herring are shut off with running twine, it is possible to set the purse seine inside the stop seine to actually harvest the fish. A large school of fish can be held behind the twine indefinitely while a few are harvested with the purse seine as needed or as can be sold.

Unfortunately, before we had the new stern in dory number three, Alden phoned and demanded that I return the *Grace Egretta*. I put him off, denying the accusations that I had stolen his boat. But when he called and announced that he was on his way to Stonington and that I had better be there with his boat, or else, I took him at his word and gathered Omega Four and a half (the half being Dave's daughter Abigail, who at fourteen was damned good at operating the hydraulics). We hustled to move the only remaining seine—the purse—into the sternless dory. Luck was with us in that the purse seine was in very good condition. Other than a few nests made by mice or squirrels, the net was in need of very little repair. My crew was somewhat dismayed that we wouldn't have the power block or the big boat to work with, but I assured them that Alden had promised to deliver once we'd made a set on some fish. And Alden had assured me that we didn't need the boat or the block until we had fish shut off.

I met Alden in Stonington, sent him off in *his* boat, and returned to the island aboard the mail boat. Then it started to rain. And it rained for six weeks. It poured night and day for a month and a half. The state of Maine set a new record for rainfall that month of June, breaking the number of inches that had held that honor since 1917.

Our introduction to being members of a seining operation had not been pleasant. We bailed and pumped rain from dories on a daily basis. One day in week five produced a particularly heavy rain accompanied by wind. It was my turn to keep the dories afloat. The weather forecast had called for easterly wind, which suited me fine as that would leave all three dories in the lee of our island, and make for easy access by skiff to pump them out. Well, the wind wasn't out of the east. And it blew much harder than expected. I watched the two dories I could see from my parents' house fill with water and begin to wallow in the building sea. It had become impossible to go alongside to dewater now that the boats full of twine were bouncing all over the place. One knock with that weight to the side of my skiff, or even the *Mattie Belle,* and I might just be swimming for shore. I was kicking myself for not pumping earlier when one of the dories began swinging back and forth until a big wave crested over its stern quarter and capsized it. Down she went, stern first. Because there was flotation in the dory, and the twine apparently got caught on the stern, it stayed vertical with the tip of the bow above the surface and pointed toward heaven. (Being the glass-half-full gal that I am, I naturally failed to acknowledge that the stern of the dory was pointed in the opposite direction.) I learned then and there that there is no more helpless feeling in the world than watching a boat sink.

The heavy rain didn't take a breather for another twelve hours. The dory we had placed in Laundry Cove sank, resting fully in the mud on her bottom. The water was so shoal where she went down, all two hundred fathoms of cork line bobbed on the surface like a giant cluster of mushrooms, and the entire dory was quite visible when I drifted over it in my skiff after the gunk churned up by the storm had settled out of the water. Understanding that the Laundry Cove mishap would be the easiest retrieval, we focused on what seemed the bigger problem: the heaven-pointing dory in Robinson Cove. I called Alden for advice on how best to proceed and let him know that I could really use that power block to retrieve two-thirds of my gear. Pulling it back into dories by hand—if we could float the dories—would be foolhardy (not to mention backbreaking). Alden agreed to come with the boat, and gave me some specific instructions about what to do while I waited.

Alden had seen it all in his many years on the water. He didn't sound surprised that two of my dories were down. He told me everything would be fine and even volunteered that he'd been in much stickier situations. Our first task was to upright the vertical dory by untying it from the mooring and towing it by its painter. Alden claimed that once the dory was horizontal, and if it was towed at just the right speed, the water would spill out over the rails and stern until it was buoyant enough for us to go alongside with our twelve-volt pump to finish the job. Bill Clark and I went out with the *Mattie Belle* to give this procedure a whirl. I pulled up to the dory, and Bill untied the bow line from the mooring and tied it to a line on my stern with which to tow. I put my engine in gear at dead idle and waited for the towline to become taut. As soon as the line was straight, the angle of the dory changed just enough to allow whatever was holding the stern down to let go, and the dory literally jumped out of the water and smashed into the *Mattie Belle*'s stern with enough force to punch a hole just above the waterline. Bill and I were somewhat stunned. To see a big boat launch itself from beneath the surface with enough velocity to deny you time even to scream or hit the deck was simply amazing. It was like a giant fish breaching. I had my usual reaction to the last straw in a string of misfortunes: I laughed. I stopped laughing when a voice on the VHF radio said, "I thought that fish was coming aboard!"

Bill and I stood looking over the transom at the damage for a couple of minutes before moving on to step two. The dory was now horizontal but upside down. Alden had said that towing the dory would right it, and we were already tied in. So we towed. We towed slow. We towed fast, and we towed at half speed. We towed on a short line. We towed on a long line, and we towed with a midlength line. We towed straight. We towed in circles. The dory would not flip over. The only thing it did do was take an occasional deep dive. Each time the bow went for the bottom, I slacked the throttle until it came back to the surface. Up and down; the dory had become a gigantic porpoise. Bill suggested we tow the dory to the town landing, where we could pull one side up with the hydraulic winch on the end of the dock. That seemed like a good idea.

In the middle of the thoroughfare, I lost all ability to steer the *Mattie Belle*. I didn't know whether I had blown a steering line or lost the pump, and there was no time to check it out. Fortunately, we were towing very slowly and Simon happened to be nearby in his boat, *Scalawag*. I waved him over and asked for a tow to my mooring. He was happy to help. After securing my boat, Bill and I hopped aboard with Simon, tied the stubborn dory to *Scalawag*'s stern, and asked for a ride to the dock. Within two minutes, the dory was easily rolled over and we were pumping her out. I decided that in the future I would listen to Bill, as he is always quite logical and extremely clever with most everything.

Later, Dave and Nate had easier success with the Laundry Cove dory, and sustained no damage. Now all we had to do was find the ends of both doryless seines and mark them so that when Alden arrived with the *Grace Egretta*, we'd be set to haul the twine back into the dories. The Robinson Cove seine was cooperative. The end was in plain sight. I tied one of my orange-and-white lobster buoys to it and headed for Laundry Cove, where I spent six unsuccessful hours. Every time I reached down and grabbed the cork line to pull to find an end, I ripped the line from the net. It was useless. I had to condemn the seine, justifying that it was too rotten to fish, and vowed to cut the corks from it and leave the rest on the bottom to totally disintegrate. So already I had a third less twine than I had started with. And we hadn't made a set. In fact, we hadn't seen a single fish.

Alden came the next day. We quickly hauled the Robinson Cove twine, placing it back into the infamous dory, and returned it to the mooring. So here we were, Omega Four, with a fresh start. The problem was, I was disheartened. My crew had to jump into their lobstering lives to try to salvage a season and make up for time and income lost while frigging with the seining operation. We all understood that the good berths for herring, or places that historically attracted fish, were all occupied by dories of fishermen from Stonington. A dory left on an anchor marks that spot as taken. It's first come, first serve. And we had gotten into the game too late to claim any fertile territory. Eventually swordfish season rolled along, and I couldn't leave the island fast enough. The herring gear that served as a daily reminder of my total failure as a seine fisherman was stored away indefinitely. We hauled the dories onto the shore below the schoolhouse and flipped them upside down (with some difficulty I might add). We stowed the twine on the float and tied it to a summer person's mooring. It was early August, and I was headed to the Grand Banks aboard the *Bjorn II* and spent two months doing something I was relatively good at. Paychecks worked in a wound-licking sort of way. And "out of sight, out of mind" with regard to the seining business rang true until February, when the whole works washed ashore right in front of my eyes, where I could not avoid it.

Of course this could never have happened in warm weather, I thought now, opening my eyes to check the level of the tide. The month of February is typically the coldest and windiest of the year. The water was nearly high, and only one end of the float wagged in the slight westerly breeze as the other appeared to remain hard aground. Westerly wind, even just a little of it, would not help. The dory was pinned on the west shore, so the wind acted to keep it there rather than assist in the other direction. This would give the folks who winter on Isle au Haut something to talk about. Our year-round population had fallen to around forty. Whether the recent decline was a cause or a symptom of certain situations that had developed in the near past, I would never know. But the island had changed. I suspected it was suffering the same identity crisis that I was. We all considered ourselves islanders above all else. And loners. In disconcertingly increasing numbers our staunch lifers were bailing after Thanksgiving, becoming virtual summer people.

I wondered now what would become of Simon and me. Our relationship had become very odd in the few months since I had begun questioning it. (Teenagers do not corner that market either.) We had been together for nearly the entire decade of my discontent, and acted sort of like an old married couple. But we weren't married, and I had just latched onto the realization that we never would be. This was depressing. Rounding into my forties, I was beginning to realize that I wasn't heading for the husband-and-2.3-children model, but that didn't mean I was content with the status quo. I knew that I needed to somehow go a separate way. But other than not marrying, and being too comfortable with each other, I had no real reason to "divorce" Simon. We had always gotten along famously. We never quarreled. We enjoyed spending time together. And now here Simon was, coming to my rescue as usual. He was always there! I just felt that we (or more accurately *I*) were missing something. I wasn't content with the reality that my primary male relationship was one of friendship.

Besides, Simon had his family, including an ex-wife with whom he remained friendly to the point of still spending what I considered a weird amount of time. And I suppose that went a long way in making me feel very much alone when I was inclined to feel sorry for myself—like now. In all honesty, my relationship with Simon's entire family, including his ex, was as easy and natural as his was with the Greenlaw clan. Regardless, settling down hadn't been what I had anticipated, and I now knew that I had been happier in rootlessness. There's not a lot of soil on Isle au Haut, so like the island spruces, residents' roots grip sheer ledge with some tenacity. Add a little rain and wind, and even the healthiest trees are prone to blow down. When "seaworthy" is the most coveted adjective in your vocabulary, life ashore is lacking. I had to admit that whatever problem I perceived in my relationship with Simon was likely a symptom of something that had more to do with me than us.

The sound of oars working methodically in locks broke my regression. I hopped to my feet to see Howard Blatchford heading toward me in his peapod, which is a small, double-ended boat named for its shape. "I brought a couple of anchors and some line," he said as he put the bow of his boat against the ledge below where I was standing. I scrambled down the rocks and climbed into the bow. I squatted down low and held both rails to balance the tippy boat. "I think we'd better run two anchors out, one off each of the offshore corners of the float, and put as much tension on the lines as we can," Howard said. I agreed that this was a good idea, as the tide was already going back out and the float wasn't going with it. The anchors would, at the very least, keep the float from going farther ashore.

Howard dropped me on the float and he rowed the first anchor to the west and dropped it in. He rowed the end of the line back to me so I could secure it to the float. He repeated the process with the second anchor, this one to the north. The two of us worked to set the anchors and get the lines as tight as we could. Of all the people who could have come to help, I thought, why did one of them have to be him? Howard was not one of my—or the island's—favorite neighbors. A known, convicted sex offender, he had served his time and come home to Isle au Haut to live out his days more quietly, adding credence to the belief held by many that our year-round population consisted largely of misfits. Ostracized for years by our tiny community, he was certainly Johnny-on-the-spot today. I wasn't exactly in a position to refuse experienced, competent assistance, no matter what Howard had done in his past. I was thankful that not many of my neighbors had witnessed this morning's collaboration. But, shamefully, not as thankful as I was for his help. And where was trustworthy Simon?

When Howard left I was happy to be alone. I spend a lot of time alone. And reflecting on that, I realized that the very things I liked most about my life were the same things I disliked. The bind I'd put myself in made it difficult to pursue significant change. The float, balanced and confused on the ledge, seemed as undecided as I was about which way to go and when to make a move. Not much of a role model. But then again, I didn't need to be anybody's role model . . . yet.

CHAPTER 3

I Am a Rock

It's staggering how much actually goes on in a tiny community while seemingly nothing is going on. All that winter, when I had chance encounters with anyone, which were indeed rare during the short days and long nights of blustery weather, there would be little news to report. "What have you been up to?" was nearly always met with a shrug and "Not much." My end of any conversation always included the thickness and quality of the ice on the island's freshwater pond, as skating had quickly become my favorite procrastination to lure me from the writing project I was falling behind on. Unseasonably warm days were challenging until someone told me that three inches of ice were enough to support a team of horses. I had no idea what that actually meant, but figured that even if the "team" consisted of just two small ponies, they outweighed me.

Spending time spinning alone on the ice was a daily ritual that I kidded myself into believing was essential for stimulation. Well, I certainly wasn't getting a lot of stimulation from people. I could go around the island in my mind, house to house, and do a head count. Every time I did, I came up with a different number. But none of these virtual trips ever produced more than forty-two fellow occupants. Even on days when the island's only grocery store (or store of any kind, for that matter) was open for a two-hour, biweekly shopping spree, I never saw more than five people. I wondered where the other thirty-seven were hiding and imagined that they must be more industrious than I was to be so busy as to not make the store hours. Even if they had no intention of buying anything, it was the best social life on the docket this time of year. I guessed, because I never saw much traffic, that my fellow islanders didn't need to fuel their cars. But they had to *eat*. And I saw boxes of groceries from a mainland market coming over on nearly every mail boat. Not that the recipients were on the dock to meet the boat and collect their food and drinks. They must come when no one is looking, I thought, and wondered why they were not as eager as I was to meet what on most days could be considered the only sign of life. And I wasn't relying on the boat for my sustenance, just activity.

Once in a while I would see someone shoveling a driveway or another getting wood for a stove, and I'd nearly scare them back to their houses with my enthusiastic greetings. Not that I wasn't normally friendly. I was. But I had never really gone out of my way for it, especially not in winter. In fact, a wave from a distance would have usually sufficed. Not now. Not this winter. Funny, I had assumed that being alone was what I needed to be productive. Everyone imagines an author in seclusion pounding the keys and tearing through the pages. This had been my mode in the past and had propelled me through the writing of all my books to date. The notion that total solitude was needed for me to perform well the job of creating written material required that I keep everyone at arm's length. I had worked to keep everyone at bay each book-producing winter, and had been unapologetic about it. I had admonished a neighbor for a friendly, unannounced visit and had hung a sign on my door, "Do Not Disturb." I had trained my family not to call me during writing hours, and I had been absolutely rude to my mother when she just couldn't wait until lunchtime to let her fingers do the walking.

But this winter things had changed. I stared at blank pages, wishing I had someone to talk to. I found myself hoping to run into Ken so that I could ask about Mariah and how she was doing at school. When I caught a glimpse of Mariah during a school break, I thought she avoided me, and excused this as her not wanting me to ask her if she was looking for any work. My newfound need to communicate must have been because I was alone more than usual; alone by choice and needing to communicate is a strange contradiction that I cannot explain. Every winter since moving to the island eight years prior, I had split time between my place on the island and in Vermont at Simon's house. When I wanted to write, I was home. When I wanted to play, I went to Vermont, where I could have fun with Simon and his group of friends. This year I had made a conscious effort to remain home as much as possible. I used my writing as an excuse not to venture anywhere or do anything that required leaving "the rock." I knew that I was looking for the exit ramp in my relationship with Simon and this required separation. So I seldom invited Simon to hang out with me. In Simon's absence, I found myself striking up conversation with anyone who made the mistake of making eye contact. My pain being self-inflicted didn't make it any more tolerable. I actually pulled my truck to the side of the road one day to chat with an itinerant laborer who had come over on the early boat to do some chain-saw work.

The man, whom I had never seen before, was leaning on the open tailgate of Bill Stevens's pickup truck, drinking from the mouth of a beat-up thermos. (Bill Stevens is our road commissioner, among other things, and often recruits muscle from the mainland to fill in where our lack of manpower needed it.) The man was dressed in heavy canvas chaps and a helmet with a full face shield that was now flipped up so that I could see his concerned look as I approached. "Hi," I said as I stopped rolling down my window.

The man spun the top onto his thermos, glanced up, and said, "Hi." I'm sure it must have seemed as if I had stopped to ask directions, which is funny considering the reality.

"Nice day for the chain saw."

"Yep."

"I'm Linda," I said with a smile that should have melted the frozen snot on his mustache. He nodded. "Are you working for Bill?" Another nod and a look of nervousness made me think he might have mistaken me for some type of authority—maybe a code enforcement officer or planning board member out on inspection, which is also funny considering the same reality. "I'm heading to the pond to go ice-skating. Have you seen that part of the island?"

"No." The man flipped his face shield back into place and picked up the saw. Before I could ask where he was from and whether he was planning to leave on the late boat, he had pulled the saw to a growling, unfriendly start, and flexed the trigger in and out in a menacing fashion. I would have bid him farewell and advised him to have a nice day if he hadn't turned his back to me. Nothing says "I'm ignoring you" quite like the roar of a chain saw.

Most of the residents weren't much more forthcoming with idle chitchat either, which is what I had always perceived as normal island winter mode, and perhaps why I had fit in so nicely in the past. Now every time I tried to strike up a conversation, I felt as though I were annoying my "target" (for lack of a better word), and usually abandoned such attempts feeling as though I couldn't approach the same person twice in a week for fear of being accused of harassment. I am certain that some considered me the proverbial fly in the ointment. Not that I was causing trouble. I just wanted to be cheerful and energetic. And those scattered demonstrations of happiness tended to put me on the suspect list. Everyone just seemed so slow, like moving through cold molasses. Most people appeared to be slightly, or in some cases, fully depressed. I knew it was a simple function of winter on the island, but I guess I hadn't noticed it as much in the past due to my own hibernation. Or maybe it was worse than ever this winter. Many people didn't venture from the front of a television set, and those who did sort of moped around lamenting their existence. Out-of-work fishermen, who composed most of the heads-of-households group, were not happy campers. Idle hands may be the devil's workshop, but my observations say the devil should have topped the invitation list.

A natural offshoot of what I was beginning to see as my personal, internal inconsistency of wanting to be alone but not wanting to be alone was the questioning of friendship, and whether I had ever experienced it. Alden, who had always been my best friend, had told me long ago that if I counted my true friends and used all the fingers on one hand to do so, I was a lucky person. Well, let's see . . . Alden is one, Simon is two. How would I define "true" friend? If I broaden the definition, I might add an old crew member or two. There were a number of summer people with whom I had become "friends." But when I recalled that some of them didn't know my name until it appeared on the *New York Times* bestseller list, "friend" was a stretch. I was well aware of all the clichés about friendship. I knew that in order to *have* a friend I had to *be* a friend. And I knew that "a friend in need is a friend indeed," and all the similar two-way-street bullshit. With this in mind, I quickly resolved that until now I hadn't needed a friend. Perhaps "need" was too strong a word for what I was feeling. But I did want a friend, and wasn't sure how to go about it.

I was battling the winter blues, too. But I refused to give in to them. I had been as down as anyone while dealing with my stranded float, which by the way did eventually drift off the ledge and in the right direction. Not as buoyant were my fellow islanders' spirits. The float and herring gear were now secured to another summer person's mooring, though Dave Hiltz had assured me, "It will never stay there." I understood this negativity as a twinge of island winter funk, and prayed that Dave was wrong. It was rumored that most of the year-round residents had been prescribed some form of antidepressant or another. If this was true, they should think about getting some better drugs, because these sure weren't working. After the school's Christmas program, I figured that the entire population was stuck in the Gordon Bok song "The Hills of Isle au Haut." That song is sung at every island function without fail. Everyone knows the lyrics, but the only verse that has any volume when sung by the community is the one about winter: "Now the winters drive you crazy, / And the fishing's hard and slow, / You're a damned fool if you stay, / But there's no better place to go." It's our unofficial theme song, and it's sung with gusto. And if you sing this winter part with some conviction, which it seems everyone does, you have no chance of being anything but depressed. We all hold dear the understanding that we are crazy, life sucks in the winter, and we are paralyzed to do anything about it because there isn't any better option. Within that scenario, gloom is inevitable.

I set myself apart from those with paralysis in that I had made a conscious decision to remain on island this winter. I had *chosen* this. I could leave at any time. The only thing holding me back from escaping to some sunny place was my personal resolution to remain here and suffer, martyrlike, with the rest of the islanders, and perhaps a bit of anticipated guilt should I actually accept Simon's offer to go away on a golf junket. I purposefully left my house and work obligations every day, looking for something—

I'm not quite sure what. It wasn't until early March that I discovered the bright spot on Isle au Haut.

I was a little bummed out to wake to six inches of fresh snow. There would be no skating today. But making lemonade with life-dealt lemons was easy once I remembered that I had retrieved my cross-country skis (among other things that had accumulated during the course of our relationship) from Simon's place the last time I left Vermont. It was early, and I assumed the plow driver hadn't made his route yet. In fact, every storm so far this winter, the driver had been somewhat frustrated by dead batteries, a bad starter, blown hydraulic hoses, et cetera. So I felt pretty safe skiing right off my front steps and planning to circumnavigate the island by road on my skis. It was a gorgeous morning, bright and crisp. I'd start on the main road to the south, I thought. My place is the last of the year-round homes going in that direction, so I would not encounter any tire tracks—just pristine, virgin snow. As I passed the drive that leads to the lighthouse, I felt a twinge of nostalgia. My family once owned the light keeper's house. I had many fond memories of spending summers in a bedroom where the walls reflected a dull, red flash of light every five seconds. But there had been a lot of snow under the skis and water under the keel since then, and I had finally forgiven the older generation of Greenlaws and had gotten over the childish grudge I'd held for so long following the sale of the family property. Could it really have been more than twenty years ago? I wondered.

Before I had broken a sweat, I was coasting down the slight

hill and around the bend after the trailhead that led to Seal Trap. Moore's Harbor was absolutely glistening. The sun was just peeking over the trees that cast long shadows on vanilla frosted ledges. The old house and barn stood erect with perfect posture that lent credibility to the granite foundations and construction methods of an era long gone. In my mind's eye I could see Carol Bergeson squatting in her garden and her husband, Lloyd, puttering with the hand pump on top of their well. I wondered how they were wintering in their off-island Massachusetts home. They were getting quite old. They always took time to visit whenever I happened upon them, I remembered. Things were different in summer. The climate was warmer on many levels. Everyone was more sociable. I coasted to a stop and took in the stunning vista while I tried to recite Robert Frost's "A Time to Talk." Frustrated that I couldn't bring it back from the depths, I continued on my way vowing to look it up when I got home.

I startled a large snowshoe hare out of hiding at the end of Anne Davidson's road. Its white fur was as fluffy as the snow it skittered over. I love rabbit tracks in their perfect triangular pattern. You can speculate on some tracks: Are they coyote or dog or some large cat? But nothing looks like rabbit tracks. The rabbit ducked under a low-hanging branch heavy with snow that clung to the needles and threatened to slide at any disturbance. If Greg and Diana hadn't gone to Arizona for the winter, there would certainly have been a beagle chasing that bunny, and a gunshot would soon follow, I thought. The only sound here now was that of my skis swishing over and through the powder and an occasional scrape on a rock. I was soon deep in Acadia National Park, which makes up nearly half of the island's acreage. Of course the park was officially closed this time of year. The two rangers were unemployed until spring. The campground was empty, the trails were all untraveled as evident from the unbroken blanket of snow at each sign marking entrances, and the float and ramp in Duck Harbor had been removed from the dock and towed to Stonington, where they were stored in the otherwise empty parking area of the Isle au Haut Boat Company.

It was easy to fall into a daydream of having the entire island to myself and imagining all kinds of grand adventures I might have if I were to be snowbound here for weeks . . . Whether at sea or ashore, I always have daydreams that include foraging for food and having to really fend for survival. Even as a kid, building forts or rafts and using slingshots or makeshift harpoons, I imagined myself as a castaway or a lone stranded survivor of some disaster. It's a quirky but fun tomboyish exercise I have never outgrown. Today's mind flex involved an avalanche. I'd have to build a snow cave, I figured. It would be easy to break branches from spruce trees for shelter, too. As I passed Duck Harbor, I thought about mussels and clams and how I might start a fire without matches or a lighter. I could eat the clams raw. I could easily spear a deer if my survival depended on it. The island is overrun with white-tailed deer, some so tame they'll eat right out of your hand. By the time I had reached Head Harbor, I had grown bored with the Robinson Crusoe game, and was feeling slightly weary from the exercise.

I was just over halfway around the island when I came to the snowbank in the middle of the road where the plow had stopped and turned to go back toward town. So the truck had started this morning, I thought. Too bad for me, as that meant I couldn't continue my circumnavigation. The only two options now were to continue around on foot, carrying my skis, or turn and go back the way from which I had come. Cross-country skiing gear was not the subject of Nancy Sinatra's song "These Boots Were Made for Walking." I turned and started back toward home—the long way. Now the day wasn't as beautiful. I started feeling guilty about the time I was spending not working. By the time I had made it back to Moore's Harbor, I was upset with myself for embarking on the circumnavigation I was unable to complete. I really needed to get on a schedule to meet a writing deadline. And that schedule would not allow for this amount of time playing. I was huffing and puffing as I ascended the last hill before my driveway. I looked up to see Kate Shaffer, my closest neighbor (only in proximity) headed toward me.

I didn't know Kate or her husband, Steve, well enough to like or dislike them but I knew a little about them, and as usual was leaping to a few conclusions. I knew that they had very recently started a chocolate-making company in their tiny home. Black Dinah Chocolatiers was named for the small mountain behind their place. I thought I recalled hearing that Kate was originally from California, but couldn't say for sure. She and Steve had been on Isle au Haut for a few years, coming at first to work as a chef at the Keeper's House, which at the time was the only B and B on the island. Kate had a reputation as a fabulous cook. When the inn closed, the couple had scrambled to find a way to make a living and remain here, which they now considered home.

California and chocolate making were both foreign to me. So I had imagined I had little in common with my neighbors. They could have been aliens as far as I knew. In spite of my craving for some verbal human contact, I planned a courteous nod of acknowledgment and hurried to pass as we grew near.

"Linda! Hi! Isn't this the most gorgeous day? I am so glad to see someone else out enjoying it!" Kate stopped, spread her arms to both sides as if embracing the western hemisphere, tilted her head toward the sun, and closed her eyes. It was as if she were meditating, which was what I would expect from a Californian. I didn't want to interrupt, so I remained silently staring at this woman who had a natural beauty, almost an aura about her. Then she suddenly snapped out of her trance and looked me in the eye. "How's the writing coming?" she asked with some genuine concern. I had grown accustomed to people asking and then not listening. As if they felt it an obligation to inquire—like asking about someone's health when they look fine and not wanting to hear if they aren't. Now Kate raised her eyebrows in expectation of an answer.

"Slow. I am having the hardest time keeping a schedule. I thought I would crank the chapters out—there's so little distraction here this winter. I think I'm going stir crazy." I smiled now at my first public admission that life was not all hunky-dory.

"Oh dear. It must be awful. I'd be going nuts too if it weren't for Steve. And Al and Kathie. And Lisa. And Alison. And Jeff and Judi." Kate might have mentioned a few other names. I'm sure she didn't mean this as a hint that I needed to make some friends. But the point was well taken. Why *didn't* I have any friends? I had fishing buddies. I had Bill Clark and Hiltzie. I had my cousin, Dianne. I wondered if a cousin was automatically a friend. "We finally have a minute to catch our breath after the Valentine's Day chocolate rush. I just got a note from Mariah asking for summer work. Can you believe the kids will be out of school in a couple months? You should come over sometime."

This was the first almost invitation I had received to do anything since the summer crowd had left. I wondered if Kate was just being polite. She appeared to be getting ready to launch back into her walk. I couldn't let her get away. It might be days before anyone else spoke to me. "Why don't you and Steve come to my house tonight? I don't know what I have to serve for dinner, but I must have something. And I have wine."

"Oh, we'd love to. But we have other plans. Let's get together sometime soon!" Kate left with a real spring in her step. I trudged the length of my driveway astonished that she and Steve had "plans." And that, I presumed, would be the extent of my social life for what remained of the winter. And I had no one to blame for that but myself. I had so successfully kept people at arm's length that if my neighbors didn't include me in their scant social calendars, it was out of respect for my privacy and work schedule. How could they know that the "Do Not Disturb" sign had been replaced by a welcome mat? I had assumed that the island's differentness in the winter was simply because it was winter. But was it the weather that made it so? Was it the lack of summer people? Or, now that Kate had mentioned the high school kids, I wondered if it was the younger generation that binds the community. In the absence of Mariah, three classmates who had graduated with her, and one the year before, only three children remained to hold down desks from kindergarten to eighth grade. And two of them were brothers, slimming family involvement in school activities to a deuce. Did the changing of seasons, the warming of weather and budding of spring, and the return of our five boarding students transform my home into a place I liked better? Or was it just my perception that had changed?

I was surprised and pleased, though, when Kate followed up on our conversation with a dinner invitation just a few days later. And just that simply, our friendship was born, a three-way bond between the married couple and me. We began spending time in the evenings either at my place or theirs, drinking a bit of wine, maybe stretching into dinner, and always sharing our hopes, dreams, and schemes. We discussed their plans to open a café at their house. The café would be a summer business, and as most of the chocolate-buying holidays were in the winter, the café would extend their profitable months. The café would be a great and much needed addition to the island! It was exciting to listen, and in fact contribute, to the couple's innovative ideas. Kate and Steve were very supportive of my work and hopes for the future, too. They offered encouragement when I felt less than productive. Their support of my work was so different from my family's favorable reception to everything. Family support can't be trusted as it is totally biased! The three of us fell into a fast and easy friendship that felt older than it was. In spite of my earlier, ill-conceived notions, I was happy to have finally added two fingers to my true friend count.

The dismal tail end of winter lingered as spring threatened

and teased with a frustrating game of hide-and-seek. My new-found rapport with the neighbors opened my eyes in a way that made me vow to never spend an entire winter alone like that again. I didn't know at the time how true to that vow I would be, or why. With the greening of spring, winter was soon forgotten. Prior to the arrival of summer folks and return of high school kids came weekend visits to the island by my sister Bif. She, as usual, accused me of living in a bubble. Naturally gregarious and liked by everyone, Bif has always been someone to whom people talk. She has a knack for charm. Her first night on the island in months, she sat at my dinner table and filled me in on all I had missed during the winter, not a stone's throw from my front door.

A teenage girl was pregnant and had narrowed the paternal possibilities down to one of two who happened to be brothers; two couples were separated and headed toward divorce; a new-comer had happened upon the island and taken up residence in a summer home (with or without permission—no one was quite sure) where it was rumored he was manufacturing drugs in the bathtub; a small association of summer residents had managed to pull off a very clever real estate bait and switch; there were reports of domestic violence; two of our fishermen were well on their way to drinking themselves to death; and our hired power company employee had supposedly staged his own death—suicide by kayak. He had disappeared without a trace, and the authorities certainly hadn't spent any time searching for his body.

"Really, Linny? Do I have to come out here to learn all of this? You've been here all winter! And we speak on the phone every day!" Bif teased. The truth was that I had heard bits and pieces of all of the scuttlebutt during the winter, but had never engaged in conversation enough to fully understand or repeat anything. Oh, and yes, I was too consumed with my own incongruity to pay attention to others'. "Mariah will be working at Black Dinah Café for the summer! Isn't that great? A café on Isle au Haut . . . It's about time."

"Yeah, I knew that," I answered in defense of what must have appeared as sheer ignorance.

So I had to acknowledge that there had been a lot going on this winter and then attempt to explain to my sister, in the face of her continual questioning, why I had denied that anything was happening now that she understood much to the contrary. Because Bif rarely visits the island between Labor Day and Memorial Day (with the exception of New Year's Eve on the millennium, which we would all sooner forget), it was difficult to explain how sticking my head in the sand, or snow in this case, had been preferable to being an integral part of the winter population. No, time had not completely stood still, as I might have falsely indicated. Yes, there had been stuff going on.

It seemed to me, in hindsight, that winter happenings were all just undercurrent. The undertow was stronger than the waves on the surface. Things below the surface are always dark, but as summer came along, this aspect was reversed. The snow receded into thin strips that eventually disappeared. The rabbits were brown again, and boats were launched. As the days grew longer and warmer, people were everywhere. Fishermen were back to work, the store was open more often and was better stocked, and all things were happier. I finished my writing project and was thrilled to be back on the water. My social life was budding with the lilacs and included both seasonal and year-round folks. The kids were out of school; those who boarded at private schools were home, including Mariah to whom I hadn't spoken in months. The young people added real spark to other changes. It was as though our island oyster world had been opened. And like a lobster in molt, we now had room to stretch and grow. Things always look better in the light of day.

CHAPTER 4

Summer Return

B ecause my parents had become snowbirds, exiting the island for Florida earlier and earlier every year, it doesn't
seem that winter has had an official end until they return,
regardless of any calendar indicating otherwise. The vernal equi-
nox might have passed on March 20, but I say spring hasn't
sprung until my mother steps from the boat to the town landing.
May 1 used to be that date. From what I understand, that ended
the year following my Mother's Day gift of a ride to Barter Creek
in my old truck to dig clams. And this year my folks didn't make
an appearance until June! So in that calendar, winter is indeed
long and spring is super short, which is fine because most Main-
ers refer to spring as "mud season." Mud season, which is as exciting as the name suggests, is something my mother has learned to
avoid. "It's just so damned gray and brown. I don't know how

anyone can stand it," she has been known to say often when trying to entice me to join Dad and her down south. And I am always tempted, sometimes giving in to temptation to the detriment
of whatever work I might otherwise feel compelled to grind out.

Work and the need to do it is something my parents once
understood. Having said that, it is also something that in their
current age has caused confusion. When my folks *do* arrive on
the island, my mother is slightly let down because, in her words,
"Vacation is over." To me, vacation indicates a break from a job
or employment, and I have often wondered what it means to my
mother. Her schedule while on Isle au Haut, from my observations,
is 100 percent social. What she could possibly consider employment, or even a light task that she doesn't also deal with in Florida,
is beyond me. Mom is somewhat of a princess. I mean that in the
nicest way. I have heard that women my age often come to a realization that they are becoming their mothers. I sure would like
to become mine. But so far it's not happening. I am a chronic
workaholic, and a tomboy to boot. Mom is neither. While I am
aware that life on an island is more difficult—everything is a
chore—it is a stretch to say that Mom works. She does keep my
father pretty busy, though. And at eighty-one, he would say that
his vacation is over when he and Mom hit the shore.

Dad's honey-do list, which is a running mental tally of things
Mom needs done, is like the bottomless mug of coffee served at
a truck stop. Every time progress is made toward the bottom of
the cup, someone fills it back up. Mom's philosophy is that Dad
will "get old" if she allows him to "sit around." If that has any merit,
I'd say that Dad has found the fountain of youth. My father

spends an inordinate amount of time under the house and up in his workshop. At Mom's insistence, and in spite of his white-collar career, my father has honed all of the trade skills to a level of competent proficiency. Dad has always been a meticulous project doer, to the point of driving insane some of us who are more of the shoddy, slam-banger type.

If Mom's vacation is over in June, she is in a very small minority. I live for June! Not only are my parents back, but so are many of my summer friends who are vacationing in the very traditional sense of the word. June is when I take the first of my buddies to arrive on island out to haul lobster traps with me and cook our catch over an open fire on the beach. And, since the Mother's Day gift blunder, June is when I now dig my first "mess of clams," or just the right amount to eat. The measure of "mess" varies wildly, depending on the strength of the back doing the digging, the number of mouths to feed, the mosquitoes, the weather, the tide, et cetera. June is often when I see the bulk of the year-round community that I may not have caught a glimpse of all winter, and teasingly accuse them of coming out of hibernation (although this particular June, the same could have been said of me). June is when the island can be held in a cool, foggy embrace that softens everything to a pale mist and muffles all but the screech of gulls working the first school of baitfish. June is when my nephews, Aubrey and Addison, proudly jig the season's first mackerel and demand that I cook it even if it looks like it's been on the dock for hours and then caught in the spokes of a bicycle on the trip from wharf to kitchen. June is when everyone waves when passing, and most stop to talk, making an otherwise ten-minute errand to the post office an odyssey. June is when the plastic, pink flamingos find Isle au Haut in their migration route and seem to be fickle about where they roost. June is when all I see of Ed White, our car mechanic, is the top of his head bobbing over the hood or his legs sticking out from under someone's temperamental ride.

The first Sunday in June is when the Island's only church begins its summer service, and when the bell rings at 10:00 a.m., I can imagine the young boys in their blue blazers and girls in crisp, white dresses gleefully pulling on the rope. June marks the beginning of a full inventory at the Island Store. Peanut butter, baked beans, and elbow macaroni make way for duck confit, truffle oil, and anchovies. Iceberg lettuce bows to endive and organic greens. Budweiser steps aside for pinot noir. White sandwich bread cowers before multigrains and baguettes, and hot dogs are upstaged by selections boasting of boneless, skinless, and prime.

This particular June hosted the grand opening of the much discussed and much anticipated Black Dinah Café. One of the most beautiful things about the café is its location. Kate and Steve's home and business is a five-minute walk from my front door. Kate is a master chocolatier. Need I say more? Black Dinah chocolates are the best, and nobody does pastry like Kate. The June opening of the café filled the void in their chocolate Internet sales and mail boat/UPS winter-shipping chaos in a nice way. The café is the first and only to offer islanders coffee and pastry and free Wi-Fi. (Until my neighbors opened their café, the only option for anyone seeking these things was sitting outside the Town Hall with a thermos.) I didn't miss many mornings of coffee and scone or cinnamon roll at the café. Kate and Steve became part of my daily morning routine as our evenings together faded.

A casual observer might note that the usual customers of the café were quite an unusual mix. But that is often the case here on the island. Our saltiest fisherman shares a table with our most noted Wall Street guy. The fisherman's wife shares warm conversation with an upper-crust summer matron. There is no elite. I feel that magic at the café every time I step through the sliding glass door. The island is the only necessary connection. Being an islander—whether year-round, summer, permanent transplant, or indigenous—levels social, financial, and ideological playing fields.

And to think that for the first forty-seven years of my life I knew Black Dinah as merely a lump, in fact a poor excuse for a mountain among a few others that cast rather short shadows on Isle au Haut or High Island. Now this relative pimple and its name denote something monumental indeed. Black Dinah is the result of a dream pursued. Hard work, perseverance, passion, and raw talent compose the entire business plan. And the chocolates . . . The chocolates are the perfect reflection of their creator. They are simply the best. Yes, this June was special indeed. And June quickly made way for July 1, the beginning of one of my favorite months.

Saturday was donut day at the café, and I knew I would need to arrive early if I expected to actually get a donut. Dave Hiltz and Bill Clark would be there waiting for Kate to get out of bed so that they could have coffee and a few of her homemade delights and get offshore before the troop of little boys (including

Aubrey and Addison) showed up to clean out the display case. I wasn't surprised to see both Bill's and Dave's trucks parked outside of the café. Nor was I surprised by the greeting I received. Dave looked at me while tapping his wristwatch. "Good afternoon," Bill said, with his usual lighthearted sarcasm. Bill's smile is infectious and his blue eyes hold a perpetual twinkle that hint of mischief.

"Geez! Must be nice to write for a living! Remember when you used to have to fish? When's the last time you were up to see the sun rise?" Dave's teasing, yet well-deserved jab was delivered from under a ball cap that had seen its share of bait and salt spray. His black goatee was always well manicured, and added a slight sinister air to his constant, fun-loving complaints. Complaining was Dave's way of communicating. That's just the way he is. "Well, you're not missing anything. Fishing sucks right now. But you're not gonna catch anything if you don't get out of bed!" July being typically one of the slower months of fishing, I knew Dave and Bill would have been offshore by now if they had good reason to be.

"I've been up for hours," I lied. "I've done a day's work before you haul your first trap." I poured myself a coffee, splashed in a lavish amount of cream, pulled out a chair, and joined my friends while I silently calculated how many days it had been since I had hauled my traps. I took a deep breath and inhaled the delicious smell of whatever Kate was concocting in the kitchen, which was hidden from view by a curtain hung in a doorway. I looked at the glass front of the large case that displayed a number of dishes full of chocolates so beautiful you'd hesitate to eat them unless you were familiar with how good they tasted. "What? Have you two eaten all the donuts already?"

"No!" Hiltz replied. "They aren't done yet. Kate is late!" He aimed this toward the curtain. "Come on, Kate! Linda is starving. She's worked up an appetite at the computer." Bill and Dave both chuckled at this while I shook my head and smiled.

"We're not open for another fifteen minutes," Kate called from the kitchen.

"Geez! What is it with you women? You're keeping bankers' hours. Or should I say writers' hours?" Before Dave could continue, a large hand pushed the curtain aside and out came Steve with a platter of donuts that were still steaming. "Geez! It's about time!"

Steve is a tall and lanky man with big hair that was just beginning to show a bit of gray. He placed the platter on top of the display case and picked up the thermal coffee urn. Satisfied that the urn was not yet light enough to warrant refilling, he put it back and cheerfully said, "Good morning! Are you all going to the meeting tonight?" Isle au Haut's town business is run by annually elected officials, one of whom was Steve. Steve was our first selectman of a board of three. It's a thankless job that pays a small stipend, and one that I have been smart (for "smart" read irresponsible and noncivic minded) enough to avoid. Small-town politics can be as brutal as any. And when you know every voter, it's difficult not to take things personally. Tonight's function was not an official town meeting, but more of a casual get-together without an agenda, hosted by visitors from Maine Coast Heritage Trust and four members of our summer community. So Steve would attend wearing only the hat of a community member. Tonight's menu was to be potluck, which means that everyone brings some food to share. Potluck is super popular on our island. I have yet to figure out why. I know that my parents would not attend, as they have a real aversion to joint-effort, buffet-style dining. But I figured I would go and give Mom and Dad the scoop the next day.

Bill and Dave both agreed that they would also attend. We sat over coffee and discussed what we thought the "real" agenda was for the meeting, about which we had been told very little. What we did know was that a large tract of land known as Bungie Head, on the southern end of the island, was for sale. It was, at the time, very unusual for property to be listed for sale on Isle au Haut. The only new construction over the span of the last eighty years had been a handful of summer cottages built on family land, and there had been a few cases when a land seeker had approached a landowner privately to pitch a purchase deal. Land stayed in family otherwise. The town of Isle au Haut owns property to sell with the intention of increasing the year-round community. Although there are some strings attached to that community-building effort, it has been moderately successful. In fact, both Bill and Dave had purchased land from the town on which to build their homes. The word that Bungie Head's two hundred acres, with two thousand feet of shoreline, were about to be placed on the open market was big news that some found disconcerting, while the endless speculation of possibilities tantalized others.

We were in the midst of the "what if" game when Kate appeared with a second platter of donuts. "I think that most people are afraid of what could happen with Bungie Head," she said. I was always amazed at Kate's graceful presence in any setting or situation. She is always very together, welcoming, and just easy to be around. She's a naturally very pretty woman who appears to put no effort into her looks. I don't know if it's her perfect posture, her disposition, her attitude, or what. But Kate is a real lady, whom most of us emulate. And her smile melts chocolate. "What if a huge developer comes here and builds condos? Or what if some wealthy single entity builds a McMansion? Either of those scenarios would do nothing to stimulate year-round growth, which in my opinion is what we need most." And I suppose that was the crux of most of our concerns: how to propel the sale of land toward building the island's community.

"Yes, but either of those scenarios might *employ* year-rounders in construction and caretaking. That would be a plus," I said. "It's nice to think about how to grow, but what about jobs for those who are here and trying to stay? I imagine that piece of property has a big price tag. It's hard to believe that Bungie Head could be purchased by anyone *without* intentions of commercial development or a plan for a huge estate. Besides, *any* construction would broaden our tax base. That's another plus." The five of us batted around opinions and ideas until Dave and Bill pushed themselves away from the table and the conversation to get aboard their boats and haul traps. Our coffee klatch discussions could go deep and broad with very little factual basis, especially those prior to a meeting of any kind. We often engage in light and harmless gossip when there is no other political intrigue to hash over. We would meet at the Town Hall this evening and have a lot more to talk about the next morning. Just as some other customers started to trickle into the café, I left to do some writing with the intention of getting offshore a little later in the day.

Things are normally slow to change on the island, but one significant and conspicuous change has been that many of our staunch summer residents have begun to rent their places out when they don't occupy them themselves. Where August and September are most coveted times for family vacations in Maine, July brings some unfamiliar faces as renters. While I recognized vehicles and knew with which cottage they belonged, I seldom spoke more than a cordial greeting with people who would only be here for a week and possibly never be seen again. Besides, it usually takes more than a one-week stay for offshore folks to get into the Isle au Haut groove. By the time renters realize that it's okay to wave to total strangers when passing, it's time for them to return to whatever city they hail from and continue the practice of keeping a close watch on the exact spot of the sidewalk where their next foot will fall. A small gaggle of renters excited by the rewards of donut day brushed by me as I left the café. It might be a rather sparse spread at the potluck tonight, I thought. Most renters would have no interest in Bungie Head.

The fog of June seemed to have cleansed the July ocean to a sparkle. I turned my laptop computer away from the glare that reflected through my bedroom windows so that I now faced Penobscot Bay. The Camden Hills perched easily on top of the lower, closer island of North Haven, which I had seen nary a shadow of in the pea soup fog bank of the past few weeks. Boats worked their lobster gear in endless, lazy circles connected by quick dashes between buoys. The surface of the water was dotted with the multicolored, bullet-shaped floats that mark the gear that was now so dense I could hear the sailboaters complaining that they "could walk on them." The very same complainers seemed to enjoy what these nuisances produced, though. I closed my eyes and saw eleven-year-old Aubrey clad in oilskins and boots that were too big for him, pulling the skiff alongside of a visiting sailboat and holding up lobsters in either hand. Who could resist buying lobster from this blond, blue-eyed boy who had hauled his traps by hand? And all-cash sales made it easy to be unable to make change. And change pocketed was that much more to put toward the dirt bike. Next year Addison would have his own traps, I thought. I love when my family is on island. I wished summer could last forever.

Addison was in my dooryard, lying flat on his belly. As I passed, I could see what appeared to be two halves of a snake connected by a very stringy piece of skin. Addison didn't look up from what he was clearly enthralled with and said, "Lawn mower. Johnny." I took this to mean that Jonathan Barter had run over the snake while mowing someone's grass. The snake wriggled as Addison touched the head, then the tail.

"That's gross, Addy," I said and kept walking.

"It's not gross. It's cool!" Gotta love little boys, I thought. I would have invited my nephew to join me in a visit to his grandparents, but I knew that even the promise of one of Grandma's blueberry muffins would not motivate him to leave the snake behind. I hesitated and considered asking him to toss what would soon be added to a long list of summer fatalities into the woods. "It's just a common garter, Linny. I mean, it's not like an eastern ribbon. They're endangered." I recalled a hummingbird that Addison managed to capture and refused to release, calling it his pet bird even after it had been dead for a week. "Just sleeping," he'd say as he stroked the tiny bird. Of course all of the adults had warned him that the bird would die if he didn't let it go. His response to this was something to the effect that the ruby-throated hummingbird lives a maximum of only nine years. So if *he* had been born a hummingbird, Addison reasoned, he'd already be dead. Before any of us could question how he knew the age of this particular bird and protest that he may well be seriously curtailing its average life span, Addy was already reciting facts about migration and number of beats of wings per second. No sense talking about the snake, I thought. Addison knew much more about it than I did. I shrugged and continued toward my parents' house.

I stepped into the house and over my father, who was lying on his side with both arms under the dishwasher. "Hi, Dad. What's up?" I asked, while I grabbed a coffee cup from the cupboard. Shepard Smith's *Around the World in 80 Seconds* blared from the other room. The endless loops of Fox News were truly endless in my parents' house, adding a strange ambience that forecast their ideological allegiances and led to mild hostility when nonbelievers dared comment. The secondary noise was the music coming from upstairs and an underlying whir of the rowing machine Mom had taken a liking to.

"Hi, Linny. Small leak. I think I have it," Dad answered.

"Your mother is upstairs. Martha! Linny is here!" Dad called loudly in an attempt to be heard over Shepard Smith, Neil Diamond, and the exercise machine.

Of course my mother did not hear this, so I walked into the middle of the living area and called up to the open loft. "Hey! How many more minutes?"

"Two more. I have to do thirty," she yelled strongly for a woman of her age who was twenty-eight minutes into what sounded like a vigorous row. Mom soon appeared above me with the same wide smile I always received when I dropped in.

"Thirty minutes? Way to go!" I cheered and pumped a fist. My mother turned the music off and skittered down and around the spiral staircase, joining me at her kitchen table.

Battling and surviving cancer twice since the age of seventy had resulted in quite a shrinking of my mother physically. She was never very big to begin with, and was now fairly tiny. But she was short, let me say, only in stature. A gigantic personality with a hugely strong mind, she would never be accused by anyone who knew her of being anything but large. She pushed her silvery gray, chin-length hair neatly behind her ears, adjusted her glasses—the lenses of which appeared not to have been wiped in many meal preparations—and said, "You're not going to that potluck tonight, are you?" I felt my eyebrows rise into high arches and I chuckled. "What?" she asked.

"Gee. You don't have an opinion about whether I should go or not, do you?" Now it was my mother's turn to chuckle. But she didn't answer. "Because it sounds like you might want to influence your forty-seven-year-old daughter's dinner choice."

"Well, you can obviously go if you *want* to."

"Thanks."

"But your father and I will not be there. Gawd, I just cringe at the thought of who and what has gone into some of the food." Now my mother shuddered as if she had just witnessed something quite gory. "Do the kids still have lice?" she asked quite pointedly. Before I answered, she asked about the confirmed case of worms. When I assured her that these isolated instances had occurred several months ago, she launched into phase two of her justification for not going. "And the whole potluck thing is so uncivilized. Who wants to eat at five o'clock? And you can't even have a drink. Not even a glass of wine." Now we were getting to the meat of the issue. Five o'clock had been cocktail time in the Greenlaw household since I was old enough to pour the Scotch. And I was doing that as soon as I could reach the ice cube trays. And when I was old enough to start consuming beginner drinks, such as fuzzy navels and Kahlua sombreros, I was advised by my mother: "If you're going to drink, drink adult beverages. That stuff you are drinking is full of sugar—too many calories! Have a Scotch." So if my mother was urging me to drink Scotch at the age of eighteen, there was little chance I could persuade her to be a teetotaler tonight and consume food that, in her opinion, had been prepared by filthy people in germ-infested environments. We had gone down this road before.

"Well, I guess I'll take one for the team. I'll go and give you a full report tomorrow," I said as I got up to leave.

I stepped over my father and wished him luck with the leaky dishwasher after my offer of help was politely refused. "You're the one who needs luck! Potluck!" Mom called over Fox News as I closed the door behind me.

Five o'clock wasn't long away, and I was expected to show up at the Town Hall with a dish to share. It was a mistake to be late to a potluck; one that you only make once. First come, first serve. There are certain island cooks whose offerings are "gulled down" way before the middle of the buffet line has helped themselves, leaving other dishes to languish humiliatingly. Nobody will eat Lee Small's boiled hot dogs. Not that it bothers Lee. At the end of the night he grabs the now room-temperature "red snappers" (with "natural" red casings that are close to the color of nail polish), and proclaims, "These little beauties will be lunch—all week." His two sons—growing boys, nearly men with healthy appetites—roll their eyes and smirk with bellies full of everything other than the snappers. I think it's not too much of a stretch to say that 40 percent of the potluck is elbow macaroni casserole. I searched my pantry and refrigerator for proper ingredients with which to sling something together in a hurry that was neither hot dog nor pasta based.

I do not recall what I contributed to the potluck dinner that night, but the facts that were dispensed are still fresh in my mind. The whole Bungie Head chapter in the book of our island will forever be thought of by me as the Bungie Head Bait-and-Switch Caper or something that implies sleight of hand. The heirs of a firmly rooted summer legacy had decided to sell off some of their inheritance. The Maine Coast Heritage Trust had some interest in purchasing Bungie Head. Its sale was brought to its attention by a small group of our summer residents who were nervous about what might happen if the land fell into the "wrong hands." My answer to "What can we do?" is, "If you're concerned about what is going to happen, buy it yourself." If the trust acquired Bungie Head, the land would go into a charitable trust, which meant that it would be removed from the island's tax base, and would never be developed in any way. Public access would be mandatory—which, for all intents and purposes, was the equivalent of extending Acadia National Park's border to include the privately owned piece currently for sale. The park now held just under 50 percent of our island—and by law that percentage cannot be exceeded because our forefathers thought it necessary to leave the town and community some room to grow. A comprehensive plan had been written and adopted back in the 1970s, and that plan spelled out a view for our future as a community. Thirty years later things hadn't changed much. The problems were still the same: The human population was shrinking while the white-tailed deer were taking over the island, and our lobster fishermen were still being squeezed by nonresident fishermen. Of course it is more complex than that, but those are the biggies.

While I was at first perturbed by the coalition of summer folks who claimed to be preserving the Bungie Head property forever and keeping it as wild and undeveloped as it had always been, I have come to envy the masterminds of the plan, wishing that I had thought of it myself. This coalition, which I will refer to as "the land pirates," ostensibly brokered a deal to sell Bungie Head to the Maine Coast Heritage Trust while carving out and securing house lots for themselves at a fraction of fair market value. Basically, the trust is in the business of buying up large tracts of land and putting them into "conservation," which means there will be guaranteed public access and no development. Once the land is in the trust, it can't be taxed. So the land pirates managed to almost steal buildable lots with the assurance that their new places would be bordered by free and wild and nondevelopable land. Pretty smart, I'd say. This simplified version, which is more a statement of my capacity to grasp it than an attempt to keep the telling painless, has had plenty of time to cool.

And to all of the arguments and questions that arose during the potluck regarding the loss of tax revenue and loss of potential jobs that could have come from some form of development, the answer was that there were now four house lots. These four lots would be built upon by using local labor. Lots would be cleared, roads would be built, septic systems designed and installed, houses constructed . . . And these four new homes would certainly pay more in taxes than the undeveloped land had. And these new homes would be connected to the local electric power grid, further bolstering the island's economy. And of course all of the materials needed for construction would be ferried over by our mail boat, which is always in need of a cash infusion. And just maybe one of the houses would be a year-round dwelling with a family of many children to attend our school. And just maybe a section of shore frontage could be obtained for the island's commercial fishermen on which to construct a dock and increase tenfold our access to working waterfront. And if we had a dock to work from on the south end of the island, surely we could win back some of the fertile fishing ground that is fished only by outsiders.

Well, the bottom line is that by the end of the potluck meeting, it was clear that the real estate transaction was a done deal and we'd better figure out how to make the best of it. It's too bad that so many of the year-rounders had such a bad taste in their mouths about it, because it seemed to me that the pirates just wanted pats on the back for jobs well done. They were somehow saving the island and getting no thanks. Saving from what or whom? I guess most of us are just too stupid to understand that part (yes, that is an attempt at sarcasm). Lee Small left with his platter of hot dogs. I left as frustrated as most of the year-round population, and wished I had taken my mother's advice. Oh sure, we had fun with the topic as a conversation piece at the café for a week or so. But it was soon August and we were on to other things.

August is thirty-one days of sheer joy! And this August began with all of the usual hoopla and held promise to pan out pure gold. The weather early in the month was stellar: days of T-shirts and nights of a blanket pulled right up under your chin. August is by far the most social month. There are cocktail parties, dinner parties, welcome parties, farewell parties, and impromptu parties that pop up like the patches of blueberries decorating the island in swatches of purple that are as festive as the parties themselves. My all-time favorite party is a "rafting up," which is basically a floating, clam-digging, fishing picnic. Rafting up is when two or more boats tie up together and share one anchor. All boats are filled beyond legal capacity with fun-loving people who are relaxed enough not to fret about the shortage of life jackets. Essentials are beer, food, a grill, an outdoor propane burner, a clam hoe, and fishing rods. This particular August my sister Bif and I organized a raft to beat all rafts: six boats and a skiff! We hosted rafters who ran the gamut of ages from eight to eighty. I laugh when first-time visitors to the island (upon learning that we have no shopping mall, movie theater, theme park, golf course, swimming pool, restaurant, or video arcade) ask, "What do you *do* here?" My answer to that is, "Follow me."

August is when the lines separating friends and family become fuzzier than usual. When Addison asks, "Is Barney my uncle?" I know how badly he wants the answer to be yes, so I confirm even though there is neither blood nor marriage to substantiate the role. The Greenlaw houses burst at the seams with family, family friends, friends of friends, pets of friends, and family of friends of family. Our mantra is the more the merrier. And yes, there is *always* room for one more. August is when the tribe of young boys swells from the usual pals—Greenlaws and Barters—to enough to make up a softball team that will take on any challengers on any given evening. August is when at least one window is shattered by slingshot or BB gun, and we are all thankful that "nobody lost an eye." The nephews often spend time with me while their parents commute on and off island to work. Sunday afternoons used to be full of tears while very young boys had to make the painful decision to stay on island without Mom and Dad or leave their island playground until the following Friday night. This August the boys barely had time to wave good-bye to their parents from the dock. The parting questions had changed from "When are you coming back?" and "Why do you have to work?" to "Do we have money on our store tab?" and "Can you bring mackerel jigs and BBs Friday?" Growing boys have access to several refrigerators on the island. Meals are eaten wherever the boys happen to be when something is served. And they sleep wherever they happen to end up when they run out of steam. The speed of the revolving doors in all of our homes increases in August. And before we know it, the month is coming to an end and we're actually looking forward to some quiet time.

Just two short months ago I was lamenting the quiet. Too quiet, I had thought. It had been a lovely summer, but I knew it was coming to an end soon and I wondered whether I would have the brass to slip the yoke and detach myself from all to which I felt tethered and face another solo winter. I had continued to work on the laces that bound Simon and me into what my family referred to as "the fun couple," making efforts to actually plan and follow through with activities independent of my friend. We were physically detached, both geographically and in sleeping arrangements, for sure. But emotionally I still felt entwined, as evident from my phone records. My sea legs were starting to twitch, ready to take strides that would leave my life on land waving good-bye from the dock as the lines were cast. As my lives at sea and ashore had drifted apart with time, the bridge that spanned the two had tapered under the stress to a thin, soft, pulled taffy–like strand that threatened to break. And I felt pressure to choose on which side I wanted to be marooned. And I knew that I would have to choose soon if I intended to line up a boat and crew to fish the Grand Banks season this fall.

Late this particular August, and early enough in the morning that I was tiptoeing around my house so as not to wake any of the overnight guests, the phone rang. I rushed to pick it up before it could disturb the nephews, cousins, and neighbors' kids who had crashed on my couch and surrounding floor. I could see from the caller ID that it was Bill Clark. It's not unusual for my phone to ring before 6:00 a.m., and when it does, I know it's one of my fishing buddies with a question or favor to ask, or some information to share. I was pleasantly surprised to hear Bill's wife, Brenda, on the other end.

Brenda is a great family friend (yes, I had reached the age where I shared friends with my folks) whom I see too little of in the summer months when we all get so busy with extended families who tend to visit exclusively when the only complaint is mosquitoes. Bill and Brenda enjoy the same family/friend equation that the Greenlaws do. In fact, Bill's father, Arnold, had come to live full-time with them, as had Bill's, son, Nate, who was a young, handsome, welcome addition to our community. Bill and Brenda's closest off-island friends had become friends of mine, too, and vice versa. Most important, the Clarks were very good friends of my parents, which, to my mind, is the truest measure of what anyone in my world is made of.

Relative newcomers to Isle au Haut, Bill and Brenda had made a bold move just a few years ago, uprooting and coming here from the Camden area. They were both freshly divorced and starting over together, committed to living on the island where they instantly fit in like lichen on the ledges. They began their island existence in a town rental house and quickly bought land and built their own place that was as warm and welcoming as Brenda herself. Their place sits close to the top of Annis Hill, where they can see clear across the bay. Their perch and watchful eye give all boaters transiting the sometimes windy gorge between the island and Stonington peace of mind. They keep a VHF radio turned on at all hours, and Bill has rescued many a broken-down boater, towline attached and no questions asked.

This morning Brenda's voice wasn't the usual cheerful half giggle I'd anticipated. She was agitated and talking very quickly and jumping in and out of sentences, leaving me with fragments of near hysteria. I stared out the windows and tried to piece together from Brenda's comments the story of the nightmare Mariah had endured last night, when the rest of us were having the best party right there on my deck. It seemed that Mariah had literally run from her house to Bill and Brenda's to escape a drunken uncle Ken, who was on her heels until she reached the big hill in front of Charlie Bowen's house, where she was able to pull away. Mariah was crying uncontrollably when she burst through their door and handed them a letter she had crunched up in her fist. Unbeknownst to anyone but Mariah, Uncle Ken had fallen off the wagon. Eventually he showed up outside the Clarks' house and put on quite a show, screaming and carrying on about wanting his girl back. His language was foul. He wanted to fight Bill, who was wise enough not to lay a hand on the very intoxicated man who could barely stand on his own. We don't have a police force on the island—we don't even have a cop—but Bill and Brenda called on two island men to escort Ken home while they consoled Mariah and promised that she could stay with them until her uncle cleaned up his act. There was no way anyone would let Mariah go home with him that night.

This had all happened, of course, a few hours before Brenda called me. Having now spilled the whole story, Brenda was at last calm enough to speak more coherently. Ken had been taken back to his house, from which he called Bill and Brenda repeatedly, threatening them and pleading for Mariah to return home. The calls continued through the wee hours, ensuring that nobody got one minute of sleep. Ken then called the county sheriff's office, which was many miles away by land and sea, and reported that the Clarks were holding his legal ward against *his* will—sort of like kidnapping. The sheriff called Bill and Brenda, who explained the situation and said that Mariah was not going back home unless the sheriff came and took her there himself. It sure sounded like an ugly, drunken drama, I thought as I stepped over Aubrey, who had slept with a leg draped over his younger brother, who slept soundly, still clutching the wooden pirate ship he'd built. This shit doesn't usually happen until midwinter, I thought as Brenda continued.

Apparently, according to Mariah, Ken had been hiding his drinking from everyone for a while, Brenda relayed. And now things had gotten out of hand. He had written a letter to Mariah that was so nasty, she was frightened enough to try to climb out a bedroom window. Much to Mariah's horror, her windows had been nailed shut from the outside. This sent the teen into panic mode. She fled her room, ran by her uncle, and bolted for the safety of the Clarks', where she had always been welcome. The Clarks had already contacted the island's visiting doctor, and he had agreed to come out as soon as possible to urge Ken to go to a hospital for evaluation and drying out. Until that could happen,

Mariah needed a place a stay. And although Bill and Brenda loved Mariah, at this time she had to sleep on a couch at their place because family occupied all the available beds. And it would probably be best if Ken didn't know where Mariah was until he could get sober and back on the right track. All of my clan was scheduled to vacate this afternoon, leaving me with an empty nest that could surely house a little bird temporarily. So, I thought, why not?

"But," I asked, "why isn't Mariah away at school? Shouldn't she be starting her sophomore year?" I had seen Mariah a few times when I had gone to the café for a late coffee (her working hours didn't begin until 10:00 a.m.). I hadn't been to the café after 7:30 lately and just assumed that Mariah had gone.

"Well, Ken found out that she had a boyfriend at school and decided that a boarding situation was not enough supervision. He's forbidden her to go back. Called the school and everything. She's enrolled at the local day school on Deer Isle and needs to be on the mail boat tomorrow morning," Brenda said. Wow, I thought. That's pretty severe punishment: taking away a kid's private, exclusive, full-scholarship education. And the local public high school requires boat rides to and from every day. Sure makes for a long day with no extracurricular activities after school. Brenda seemed uncomfortable with my silent digestion of all of this and added, "Ken hacked into her e-mail, and, well, he's in bad shape with the drinking. His reaction to the boy thing was totally inappropriate." Yes, I thought, I had been instrumental in getting Mariah to apply to boarding school because it is a great opportunity. She must be . . . fifteen. Isn't it normal to have a boyfriend at that age? Hell, Aubrey is only eleven, and he's noticing girls. I wondered briefly whether this was a situation where a mountain was being made of a molehill. Ken would probably sleep off his drunkenness and everything would be back to normal by this afternoon. Maybe I would suggest that Brenda and Bill keep Mariah until Ken comes to his senses. Did I really want to be involved in this bullshit? Everyone needs a good night's sleep. That's what my mother would say. A good night's sleep will brighten up any bad situation.

As if reading my mind, Brenda continued. "Listen to this letter he gave her." And she read.

Mariah, it doesn't seem likely that things will ever be the same between us, as they once were. There are too many negative feelings that have built up over the years. It seems like I don't have anything to say to you anymore, because of what you did at Evergreen. I'm sorry for that, but I can't help the way I feel. Now we're at the point where I can't even SAY the way I feel, because you'll go running to tell Bill and Brenda and make yourself look like the victim. Let me remind you that NONE of this is MY fault. I'm not the one who did something wrong.

When I was talked into letting you continue to live here, it was on the condition that you would make some changes in your behavior. You said you would break your ties with the friends who were a bad influence, but you haven't done that. If you were serious about that, you would have removed them from your Facebook and MySpace, but you did not.

Cowgirl [that's Mariah's cat, Brenda said] *brought your Hello Kitty pouch out from your room the other day and was attacking it. It was full of your stash of small-dick condoms. After I stopped laughing at how small they were, it occurred to me that the fact that you KEPT THEM shows that you have no intention of changing your behavior. A person who isn't planning to have sex doesn't keep a stash of condoms hidden in her room. And no, you are NOT allowed to have condoms. If you are going to continue to suck cocks and fuck, then you can pay the price for doing that, whether it's AIDS, herpes, or pregnancy. [Nasty drunk! Brenda fumed now.]*

Before I realized those things, trust was zero. Now it is LESS than zero, if that's possible. I don't think you can earn that trust back, and it looks like you're not even going to try. I really don't get why you want to stay here. It's not going to be pleasant for either of us. Why on earth do you want to keep living here? Don't you know how it is? Can't you figure it out? Almost everyone on the island looks at you now and imagines you spreading your legs for the Evergreen boys. How can you stay here when you know people see you like that? Ken

Brenda sniffled a bit. My stomach turned. "What time are you bringing her over?"

CHAPTER 5

Storm

Things progressed that day at the most unislandlike speed. Brenda called to say that the doctor and the sheriff and our local minister were headed out to visit Ken in hopes of persuading him to get some help. The next call confirmed that Ken had gone along peacefully enough to be admitted into a hospital in midcoast Maine, where he would consent to an evaluation and whatever appropriate treatments were necessary to get him healthy again. Perhaps he'd been down and out before and was admitting defeat. This was positive, I thought. Now that Ken was not there, Bill and Nate would take Mariah home to collect a few things and deliver her to me to remain under my roof and care until Ken could return sober and take responsibility for his niece once again—a couple of weeks at the most, I figured. There was a strange, unspoken wondering among us about what else could have transpired under Ken's roof, but I guess we really didn't want to know. When I relayed the story to my mother, she groaned and rolled her eyes, indicating that she suspected there was more to the story. But I was able to shrug off my mother's silent suggestion. As I was now reminded, she had not liked the whole Ken/Mariah scenario from the beginning, referring to Ken as "the funny uncle."

The care component of Mariah wouldn't require much work on my part. She could stay in my downstairs guest bedroom, which has its own bath—plenty of privacy for a teenage girl. My bed and bath were upstairs, so we wouldn't disturb each other in the least. I would feed her and drop her off and pick her up at the town landing at appropriate mail boat times. Maybe I would have to buy a few groceries so she could pack her lunch for school. I'd ask Brenda what Mariah liked to eat.

That day was a particularly hectic one, to boot. Everyone who had been visiting or summering on Isle au Haut with school-aged children was packing up and bailing out. It's customary to wait until the very last minute to leave the island for the summer, ensuring that the late boat will be full of sad people who all stand in the stern facing aft as the boat pulls away from their beloved island, waving enviously to those lucky few who get to stay into autumn and beyond. My family and friends were all busy stripping beds, deflating air mattresses, rolling up sleeping bags, cleaning out refrigerators, and packing duffels. We had gathered at my house to say our last farewells until Columbus Day weekend, when the final house close ups would be done for the winter, when into my driveway came Bill and Nate with Mariah between them in the front seat of Bill's truck. I had informed my family of the situation as well as I could with the young kids around, so I was careful not to say too much in the presence of what my grandfather used to refer to as "little pitchers with big ears." It was immediately obvious that Addison had heard too much when he asked me, "Why is Mariah coming to live with us?" I nearly laughed at his use of the word "us," as his house is actually next door to mine. But I love the fact that all of our houses are indeed his.

"She is going to stay with me for a little while until her uncle gets out of the hospital."

"Is she my cousin?"

"No, honey. She is our special friend." This seemed to satisfy Addison, who now ran to open the door to let Mariah in. Addison immediately threw a big hug around a very surprised Mariah and explained to her that he had to go home to school but that he would be back every weekend. Kids are funny, I thought, and very perceptive. I figured Mariah would be back in her own place by the next weekend, but Addison was so intent on everyone he liked being part of his family network that I let it slide in spite of the fact that I assumed Mariah would be unhappy about the prospect of staying here that long.

The crowd left to catch the boat, leaving Mariah and Bill and Nate and me to stare at one another in silence. When it got so awkward I couldn't stand it, I started jabbering nervously. "Okay. Well, welcome, Mariah! God, you've only been to my house in the past to collect paychecks. Let me show you around. This is the kitchen . . ." While I was in the midst of showing a dazed girl how to operate a toaster, which she no doubt understood better than I did, Bill and Nate suggested that they bring in Mariah's things from the back of the truck while I completed the house tour. I showed her everything! I heard my front door open and close several times, but it wasn't until we emerged from the laundry room tutorial that I realized how much stuff this kid came with. Everything was in open, rectangular, plastic fish boxes, which are normally used to carry lobster to market or bait to boats. And there were many boxes. It looked as though the three of them had thrown everything they could get their hands on into the plastic totes as fast as they could. I was tempted to ask if Ken's house was on fire while they were there, or whether they were afraid of getting caught "stealing" her things. What a mess! I caught Bill's attention with wide, questioning eyes.

"Well, you know teenagers," he said. "They need lots of clothes! Only a couple more totes, and we'll leave you alone." He and Nate left to grab the last of the boxes that topped off a huge pile in the middle of my living area. Really, I thought, this looks like every piece of clothing the kid ever owned. There's no way she could possibly wear all of this. Then I noticed three boxes of books.

"Planning on doing some reading?" I asked.

"We didn't know what she'd need. And Ken's place is a mess. We didn't want to have to go back and forth too many times for things she forgot, so we just brought it all," Bill said, in a matter-of-fact way.

"Okay, cool," I said, not wanting to go any further with a conversation that might be uncomfortable for Mariah or indicate that she was unwelcome because of all of her belongings. "Let's move some of the things you won't need right away to the basement, shall we?" Mariah was in charge of putting the boxes into two piles: one that needed to be moved to her bedroom and the one of nonnecessities to go to the basement storage area. The pile of boxes for storage was rather tiny. She *needed* most everything, so the bedroom was a bit crowded. I couldn't help noticing the stench coming from the boxes—and it wasn't fish or bait. Mariah's clothes reeked of cigarette smoke and cat urine. I asked if we should move some of the clothes she wanted to wear to school to the laundry room. She agreed that that was a good idea and confided that when she had arrived at boarding school last year, she had been accused of smoking, which she assured me she did not do. I wondered about what she was accused of that might account for the cat pee, but didn't ask.

Bill and Nate left after they had given Mariah hugs and told us to "have fun!" That seemed more of a command than Bill's usual good-bye, and one that neither Mariah nor I expected to be able to accomplish. She never mentioned anything about how she felt, and I wasn't about to ask. But I imagined all sorts of good reasons for her silence. She was exhausted from lack of sleep and somewhat shell-shocked by the drama of what she had lived through in the past twenty-four hours. She was distraught about not returning to Evergreen Academy. She was upset about having to go to the local high school, where she "couldn't even have friends because of the boat schedule," the only thing she verbalized. I was sure she was embarrassed and humiliated that her uncle had taken it upon himself to tell everyone he'd run into in the last few days that she was not returning to Evergreen, and why. And she was naturally uncomfortable moving in with me, with whom she hadn't been particularly close in the past. And she was scared to death about what the future would hold. I would imagine that fear was the biggest emotion she was experiencing. The fear of the unknown coupled with exhaustion can lead to very bad thoughts of doom in any of us at any age.

But these were all my thoughts, not her words. Anything I said was met with a shrug. Every question I asked was responded to with an "I don't know," "Maybe," or "It doesn't matter to me." Mariah didn't seem to feel very strongly about anything, and I eventually realized that I was annoying her by trying to communicate. After an hour or so of staring silently into space and trying to figure out what to say or do, I decided that I needed to get out of the house. The poor kid just wanted to be left alone, I thought. I told Mariah to make herself at home and asked what I could pick up at the store for her school lunch. "I like turkey and cheese sandwiches," she said, much to my delight. I dashed to the store and bought enough to make sandwiches for the week, thinking that if Ken returned home in a couple of days, he certainly wouldn't have thought of buying groceries in his current state.

Ken's antics were the talk of the town, which was no surprise considering that our island is very seldom visited by law enforcement. We don't have any authoritative person, team, or unit, and I suppose that is because situations requiring law enforcement are so rare. Everyone I ran into was relieved that Ken, who was generally well liked and thought of as a productive resident and community member, was getting squared away at the hospital. In hindsight, I realize that many of us were sweeping the obscene letter under the rug because we didn't want to think about the possibilities. And everyone was genuine in thanking me for housing Mariah in Ken's absence. It wasn't until a few of the island women suggested that Mariah might benefit from some professional counseling that I realized that this was more about helping out one of our island children than it was about doing a favor for Bill and Brenda. The women surmised that Mariah had been bounced around a bit in her earlier childhood in Tennessee, and Ken's explanation of what he had saved her from by bringing her to Maine, including poverty, drugs, and family he described as "white trash," rang true with all suppositions. Mariah's biological mother had not only allowed her daughter to move far away, but also had consented to giving Ken legal guardianship of Mariah, making it quite clear that this was a permanent arrangement. "Who gives their kid away? That has to be traumatic! She should see a shrink." Although I listened intently to all suggestions, and in fact agreed that Mariah might benefit from some professional help, there was no way I was sticking my nose any further into her business than was absolutely necessary. I was housing her because Brenda and Bill's house was already full. Setting up and getting her to some kind of doctor's appointment was out of the question. That ball was in someone else's court, I thought.

Three days of the same routine had me feeling like a robot. I got up early, made Mariah's lunch, woke Mariah up, watched Mariah eat cereal, drove Mariah to the boat, worked until three in the afternoon fishing and/or writing, picked Mariah up at the boat, watched Mariah watch TV while I cooked dinner, ate in silence, advised Mariah to get some sleep, and went to bed. Our sleep schedules were not in sync, to say the least. Mariah was a night owl, while I was more of an early-to-bed-and-rise person. Everything was very consistent, including what I perceived as extreme unhappiness in my household. Mariah was miserable. She wasn't mean or bitchy, but she moped in sadness.

On day four I got word that Ken had released himself from the hospital, perhaps a bit prematurely. But as he said, he had every right to leave when he saw fit to do so. However, none of us were eager to find him suddenly among us again. Patient confidentiality be damned! Brenda had connections and feelers out statewide to keep us posted on anything and everything that had to do with Ken's location and status. According to Brenda, who was in daily contact with the nearest deputy sheriff, Ken had entered into some agreement with some party that to this day remains fuzzy to me. He had agreed to attend alcohol counseling once a week along with taking a prescription medication that would make him violently ill should he choose to imbibe. He was also forbidden by the sheriff to see or contact Mariah without her consent. He could call me and ask to speak with Mariah, but could do nothing more until she was ready. He had to be careful to notify me if he planned to ride the mail boat so that I could let Mariah know, or ensure that she would not be on that same boat. This all seemed quite reasonable for a smooth transition. The agreement and with whom Ken had made it must have been nonbinding, because it appeared to be very casual. Thinking back on it now, the whole arrangement was way too casual and even sloppy, and how were we going to enforce it anyhow? After all, I didn't have any legal standing in the matter as far as Mariah was concerned; I was just putting her up for a few days and acting as a kind of informal conduit for information. The agreement amounted to concessions made by Ken in exchange for something—at the time, I didn't know what that might be, but I suspected that Ken just wanted to go along with whatever was required for him to wiggle out of his legal predicament in the hope that his abhorrent behavior would blow over and he could get Mariah back into his house.

When Ken arrived on the island four days after his removal, he sent me an e-mail thanking me for taking care of Mariah and promising that he was indeed getting his act together and was eager to have his niece home. He asked permission to call me, which I gave. When he called, he was sincere in his gratitude and wanted to set a date for a reunion with Mariah. Ken suggested Sunday of that week, which was one week from the day Mariah had arrived at my place. That sounded good to me because I was eager to get back to my normal routine and thought it best that everyone else do the same. When I picked up Mariah at the boat that afternoon, she did not take the news of her Sunday reunion well. She burst into tears and said, "I'm not ready. He's not ready." She cried herself to sleep that night in spite of my telling her that the reunion could be postponed.

On Friday, after I dropped Mariah at the boat, promising to be there to pick her up at four and to inform Ken that she would not be reuniting with him as soon as he would like, I sent Ken an e-mail to let him know that Mariah wasn't feeling that she would be ready to see him on Sunday. I asked if he thought Wednesday might be acceptable. He said that he understood and wanted Mariah to be comfortable with coming back, although he was missing her. They were each other's only family now, and he wanted to take charge of his responsibility as soon as she consented. We talked about teenagers, and agreed that it would be an awkward time for Mariah even if she had a more functional, normal situation.

When I informed Mariah that Ken and I had agreed that she could use more time to adjust to the idea of a reunion, she seemed relieved. But when I heard her crying again that night, I knew it was time to listen to the advice of the island women and try to get Mariah some help. The weekend was unpleasant. I worked at my desk in my bedroom while Mariah lived on the couch downstairs. The TV was going constantly, but it didn't appear that she was watching it. She had her iPod speaker stuck in her ear, her computer on her belly or at her side, and she was reading a book. When she wasn't engrossed in the book, she was curled up in a near fetal position and dozing. She must have shifted to her bedroom at some point well after I had gone to bed, because when I made coffee in the morning, she had vacated the couch and I could hear the TV in her bedroom. She didn't emerge from her bedroom until noon on Saturday and Sunday, which I knew was typical of her age group. But I could only chalk off so much of this to typical teen behavior. It seemed to me that Mariah was suffering from real depression. I hadn't been around teenage girls since I had been one, so I could not really relate to anything she might think, feel, or express. We didn't talk. Mariah did perk up a bit when Brenda called to chat with her and invited us to dinner. And I decided I would use this chance to raise the idea of

Mariah's getting some professional help; I knew Bill and Brenda would support the idea, and Mariah trusted them.

Much to my relief, dinner over at the Clarks' went well. Mariah opened up a bit with some conversation. She was clearly comfortable with "Grammy and Grampy," as she called them with old familiarity (though it caught me by surprise—Bill and Brenda are just barely older than I am, so they were a bit young to have a teenage granddaughter, even in Maine!). Although Mariah's conversation was mostly negative about how she detested public high school and missed Evergreen Academy and all of her friends there, at least she was animated in her protests. She had a little spark that I hadn't seen. I figured the timing would never be any better, and broached the subject of counseling. Bill and Brenda both chimed in that it was a wonderful idea as if on cue, which they were not. They added that counseling certainly wouldn't do any harm, and in fact it might be good for Mariah to talk with someone who was more objective than any of us could possibly be. Mariah reacted in her usual nonenthusiastic way with a half shrug and said, "Whatever." I took that as half-assed consent, and promised to do some research and make an appointment as soon as I could get her in.

The following Monday, right after dropping Mariah at the boat for school, I started making calls to get a recommendation for a counselor. By noon that day I had an appointment set up for the very next afternoon for both Mariah and me to meet with a woman in Rockland who specialized in "teen trauma." Perfect, I thought. As Rockland is two hours from Mariah's school, the scheduling required that she miss a couple of classes, which was the only good news in her mind. I took myself ashore in the *Mattie Belle* and drove to the high school, where Mariah was already outside and waiting for me. She climbed into my Jeep, cranked up the radio, put her seat back, and fell asleep. She napped the entire ride. This didn't surprise me as I knew she was sleeping very little, if at all, at night. Maybe this meeting would help her sleep a bit, I hoped. And maybe this woman would help Mariah feel better about moving back home with her uncle tomorrow as planned so that my life could get back to normal (for me, which is far from anyone else's standard of normal). Ken had been quite understanding about the extra time at my place, but was insistent that "the crisis is over." He wanted his life to get back to normal as much as I did. I knew that routine is best in most situations, and couldn't help but believe that Mariah would be better off in her usual routine than she was with me. She couldn't be any more miserable, that's for sure.

We found the counselor's place of business without any trouble. I remember holding open the front door for Mariah to enter. She resisted, insisting that I go first while she held the door. We sat uncomfortably in a comfortable waiting room, Mariah chewing her nails while I regretted dragging her there. A woman appeared from down a long hall and introduced herself as Lesley. Lesley suggested that Mariah and I both come to her office, as this first meeting would be more informative and thus more helpful to her if she could speak with both of us. What the hell, I thought, though I hadn't anticipated participating in the session. I reluctantly followed Lesley, with Mariah trailing behind, down the hall and into her office. Lesley asked us to have seats wherever we wanted. Mariah looked at the door. I grabbed a rocking chair. Lesley offered tea, which I accepted although I don't enjoy it much. Mariah shook her head, indicating that she would not like any tea, and got very busy playing with a dollhouse. She moved miniature furniture around until she had totally redecorated while ignoring all questions Lesley asked. I had shared all that had transpired in the Ken drama over the phone to Lesley. She spent a few minutes recapping all she understood, and asked a few questions accordingly. I sipped tea, tried to field questions for Mariah (most of which I didn't have answers for), and wished I had stayed home. This was really embarrassing, I thought. I had begged Lesley to see Mariah on short notice. And now it looked as though we were all wasting time. Mariah wouldn't even look at Lesley. She basically kept her back to the woman in the rudest manner.

I was just about to suggest that we'd had enough when Lesley asked a rather odd question. "Mariah, do you have privacy in the bathroom?"

Mariah exhaled loudly, showing her impatience with this whole gig, I thought. I wanted to crawl under the couch. Mariah turned and faced Lesley for the first time in the fifty-minute session. She looked the woman squarely in the eye as I cringed and braced for whatever ill-mannered response she was preparing to launch. "No. No, I don't. My uncle has a hidden camera in a radio in the bathroom. I have seen pictures of myself showering on his computer."

CHAPTER 6

Mariah's Story

And she didn't stop there. With no more prompts, Mariah poured it all out in heart-wrenching, jaw-dropping, horrifying detail. Torn between tears and puking, I wanted her to stop as much as I wanted her to go on. Here was the story none of us had thought to look for or, perhaps, wanted to know.

Mariah's mother had given birth to her when she was nineteen. Mariah's "relationship" with Ken had begun years before when they both lived in Tennessee. They were not related by blood; Ken was the brother of Mariah's stepfather, so he was "uncle" only in the most indirect way. Ken had collected Mariah from her mother every Friday afternoon and kept her for the weekend at his house, beginning when Mariah was about seven. "My parents didn't have much money, and he bought me toys—anything I wanted." So, it seemed, Ken had been grooming

Mariah for some time, I began to realize. And what could her mother have been thinking? "I slept with him in his bed—there was nowhere else for me to sleep." I couldn't believe what I was hearing. I wanted to run away as much as I wanted to stay. I felt myself go numb. "He apologized for the pictures I saw of myself on his computer. They were taken accidently. Since then, I always take my clean clothes into the shower stall with me because I don't know where the camera is." My stomach turned when I remembered how Brenda and I had lectured Mariah about personal hygiene and suggested she bathe more frequently. "When he knew that I had seen the pictures, he gave me a credit card and let me buy stuff on the Internet." Mariah continued with an explanation of how Ken had talked with her about the birds and the bees—which was a detailed account of his own sexual exploits, including why most of the women in his past refused him anal sex because of the size of his penis. These talks happened the past summer during breaks taken from driving lessons (which she explained only took place in the national park, where there was little or no traffic to interfere with a beginner behind the wheel). Oh God, where would we start? Should I tell her now that it is inappropriate for a fifteen-year-old girl to sit in a man's lap while learning to drive? Should I explain to her that the advice to parents to talk to their kids about sex does not include show-and-tell?

Mariah had now moved from the dollhouse to a coloring book and crayons. She colored a page from Cinderella, never looking up but still talking. "And now he's e-mailed naked pictures of me to some of my friends at Evergreen and made it look like I sent them! They are calling me porn star." Waking up from a nap on the couch to find Ken masturbating while looking at her was commonplace. Ken pleaded with Mariah to wear tight jeans. No wonder she preferred baggy sweatpants. "Every time I don't do what he wants, or if he gets mad at me, he says he'll send me back to Memphis and I'll never see my friends or the island again." Her voice trailed off as she put finishing strokes on Cinderella's gown.

I wondered how bad the Memphis situation might be if she preferred to stay with Ken. Lesley asked about the night Mariah bolted from the house. "Well, he was drunk. And the air was . . . Well, it was just so thick that . . ." Mariah seemed to be searching for words. Lesley suggested a few options ranging from uneasiness to terror. "Yes. Sexual tension. I just couldn't take it anymore. I was scared and when I tried to go out my bedroom window, it was nailed shut. I knew I had to run. So I just did it." There was a long silence while Mariah turned the page of the coloring book and began a new picture. Lesley talked softly and calmly, but her words for Ken were harsh. It was clear that Mariah was done talking. I sat paralyzed.

"Well, I hope you'll understand that I am obligated to report this to the state," Lesley said matter-of-factly. I shook myself out of numbness long enough to ask how the system would work from this point forward and what Mariah and I should be doing, and what we could expect. Lesley informed me that protocol required her to report these abuses to the Department of Health and Human Services, and that they would get the proper authorities involved. She noted that nothing would happen as quickly as any of us would like and that we should go on as we had been, as well as we could, and that I should not allow Ken to lay eyes on Mariah under any circumstances. We should keep all of this as quiet as possible and allow the authorities to do their jobs. "And I hope you'll come back for another appointment next week." Mariah rolled her eyes and gasped in disgust at the prospect of returning. I was sure that she felt she'd shared all she could and had no intention of going any further. It wasn't until Lesley got up and opened her office door that I realized Mariah and I had to leave. We had to go home now. We had to ride in my car together for two hours. For once, Mariah moved faster than I did. I thanked Lesley and headed for the parking lot.

Mariah was quick to put her seat back and close her eyes. My hand was shaking as I reached out to pat her arm. She quickly pulled away, seemingly repulsed by my touch. I wasn't sure what to do, but blurted out, "I have to call Brenda. I'm going to tell her everything."

"Okay," was all I got in return.

"I have to tell her *everything*."

"That's fine."

"And I have to call my sister Bif."

"Okay."

"But that's all. I won't tell anyone else. You can tell whomever you want, but let's wait until the state takes over. It'll have to be a secret for now. And forever if that's what you want. It's up to you."

"Okay."

I was nervous as I waited for Brenda to answer the phone. I

prayed that she'd pick up, and finally she did. Brenda recognized my number, and answered with "Well, hello there! How did it go?" I told her everything as quickly as I could. I couldn't wait to get this off of me and onto someone else. Brenda cried. She relayed things to Bill as well as she could. When there was nothing else to say, Brenda asked that Mariah and I go to their house when we got back to the island. I told her that it would be late. She said they'd be up.

I called Bif, from whom I keep nothing. She was pretty shaken up by the whole story but spoke rationally. She assured me that everything would be fine and that the state authorities would handle the situation. I promised to call when Mariah and I got home. As soon as I hung up, Mariah asked, "Is what Ken did really bad?"

"Oh yes. It's really bad."

"Do you think he's going to be in trouble?"

"Yes. He is in serious trouble."

"Well, I knew some of it was wrong, but I didn't know it was *that* bad." She hesitated for a moment, as if contemplating and not sure whether to share something. "There is one thing that Ken can hold against me," she said cautiously. "I did something, too. What if he tells?"

"Mariah, you are a child. There is nothing you could have done that you'll be held responsible for. Your uncle is a pedophile and child pornographer. You are the victim here. I don't care what you've done. No one else will either." Mariah proceeded quite cautiously, as if she didn't trust me. She spoke slowly and chose her words carefully. The bottom line was that Mariah had taken pictures of herself nude at the age of eleven and had e-mailed them to a boy named Cody, with whom she had been communicating, apparently inappropriately. She said that Cody had threatened to forward all of their correspondence to her uncle if she did not fulfill his request for photos. I assured Mariah that this was nothing to worry about because she was only eleven at the time. But inside, my guts were churning. Until this afternoon, I had bought Mariah's casual response to Ken's behavior—including his alarming letter. As far as I could tell (or wanted to look), she hadn't considered the sending of nude pictures a big deal, or anything more than perhaps an embarrassment. In fact, it seemed almost like normal behavior to her; didn't everyone's guardian do that? But I knew that there was a much, much bigger and uglier thing happening here.

We arrived at Bill and Brenda's after Bill's dad had gone to bed. Nate was out with friends. The smell and sight of whoopee pies fresh from the oven made my mouth water. The heat from the wood pellet stove chased the cool, damp boat ride out of us. Or perhaps it was the warmth of Bill and Brenda that smoothed the goose bumps. Mariah shivered and snuggled up close to Brenda, who draped a strong, protective arm behind her neck and around her shoulder. We sat at the kitchen table and speculated about the future. That table had served me many a restoring glass of wine, fed me comforting dinners, and hosted hearty laughs. Midway through our conversation, the juxtaposition between now and then became as abrupt as granite steps jutting from moss. I felt as if my being there with the present mission spoiled the coziness of the Clarks' home. The ugly talk managed to dissolve their home's snugness as if someone had pulled a drain plug from the middle of the hardwood floor. Comfort flowed out of the room like mascara on the *Dr. Phil* show. It was a mess. And we tried to make sense of it.

The adults agreed that for the time being we should keep Ken's reprehensible activities very quiet. We surmised that if Ken were tipped off that the beans had been spilled about his abuse and illegal exploits, he would certainly destroy any incriminating evidence. Mariah should remain with me so as not to raise any suspicions and, of course, for her own well-being. I thought I could simply put off the reunion for as long as it would take until Ken was arrested. "And," Bill added, "if any of the guys hear about this, they'll kill the bastard. It's all I can do not to take care of him myself." I knew this was true. It's just the way islanders think. Take care of your problems yourself. Four island families had young daughters who had enjoyed sleepovers with Mariah at Ken's house. Had Mariah's friends showered there? Although I sort of liked the idea of Ken "falling overboard," it wouldn't be fair to Mariah not to have him prosecuted. And this creep was not worth someone else's going to jail for murdering him. No, death was too easy. And once he was out of the picture, we could make some arrangements for Mariah, we thought vaguely.

The doors of my house were locked for the first time ever that night. I put a sign on the inside of the front door, reminding me to unlock it in the morning as I had no key and didn't want to lock myself out. After Mariah went to her bedroom, I dug out my shotgun and some shells from a closet, loaded it, and propped it in a corner where I could grab it if needed. I lay on top of my bed and stared at the ceiling with all of the lights on. How could this have happened here, on *my* island? This place is a paradise where kids need no protection beyond helmets and life jackets and bug repellent and sunblock. How would the news of a predator in our community who preys upon innocence affect us? Would the fabric of the island be stained permanently by this? Will this be a loose thread that could unravel the entire form into a chaotic heap? Will we islanders still have the natural instinct to claim this place for ourselves and long to be claimed by it? The knowledge of what had been happening right under our noses would certainly cause everyone to question many things that we had taken for granted. "Pristine" would no longer be an adjective for what felt sullied to me now. I couldn't believe that I had locked my doors. I couldn't turn the lights out. But, I realized, for the first time since she'd come to stay, I didn't hear Mariah crying herself to sleep

About that lock—well, Mariah and I got good at breaking into the house in the days and weeks that followed. Even the reminder note on the door couldn't erase so many years of no locks, no keys, and no worries. I also got good at giving Ken excuses for Mariah's not being able to return to his care. All of our contact was by e-mail, with the exception of a few phone conversations which were preceded by an e-request for a call. Ken was definitely staying within the walls of his house. Anytime I had occasion to do a drive-by, I would sneak a peek into his home, which was easy with the huge window right in front. I never saw anything other than the TV set and lights on at night. Brenda could have been accused of harassing the state police with her constant calls to learn when someone might be coming out to take Ken away before he got nervous or got dead if word leaked out about his activities. Mariah and I went through the motions. Or at least that's what I remember of what we were doing.

The Department of Health and Human Services was the first state agency to get in gear. They called and informed me that in order for Mariah to remain with me temporarily, rather than go into a foster care program, which was the normal procedure, someone would need to visit to ensure that my place was adequate and a safe, healthy environment. The woman who would visit and check me out called and suggested that I have some of Mariah's "support" around for her to meet also. My perspective, which was admittedly naïve about this brand of proceedings, was that the process was alarmingly casual. I had seen the official paperwork from the state of Maine declaring that Ken was Mariah's legal guardian. But other than that one document, there was nothing else. All I knew of the biological mom was rumor, and I assumed that had been generated by Ken when he was looking for support and pats on his back for stepping up to care for his niece.

The social worker, Gretchen, arrived on a morning boat in midweek, which worked well as Mariah headed off to school on that boat's return trip to the mainland. I had several island women at my kitchen table, all of whom except Brenda knew only the short version of the story, which was that Mariah was staying with me until Ken was healthy and sober enough to care for her again. Before all this, I had thought of them merely as fellow islanders, and not really friends at all, but they had come in support of Mariah and her need to stay with this island family.

The women ran the gamut from grandmothers to the childless—but all hearts were in sync.

After some discussion and lots of coffee, it became clear that somebody should place a call to Mariah's biological mother to make her aware that her daughter was now staying at my place and why, and it seemed that that somebody was going to be me. As with every aspect of Mariah's case, there was some confusion surrounding the protocol. The social worker had a folder that contained a document that Mariah's biological mom had signed relinquishing guardianship to Ken. Ken had apparently done some research into the bureaucracy, and had been receiving a welfare check for seventy dollars a week from the state of Maine via Tennessee. The folder held paperwork that showed that the guardianship case and welfare receipt had been done pro bono by an attorney who happened to summer on the island. For a second I bristled at the lack of research the attorney had done and how he would feel when the truth got out. But just as quickly, I recalled that the whole community had been duped. Now that Ken was unfit, shouldn't the biological mom have the option of caring for her daughter? The state had funds with which to transport Mariah home, but they didn't seem to be in any hurry to put her on a bus.

From the social worker's folder came a slip of paper on which a number was scrawled. All eyes turned to me. I was extremely nervous, having no idea what to expect, and assumed that bio mom would be shocked and horrified and would insist that her daughter be returned to her pronto. I dialed with proverbially crossed fingers. My phone was on speaker so that both Gretchen and I could communicate with the mom, Gretchen to answer any legal sort of questions, and I because, well, her daughter was living in my house under my care, so I seemed to be in charge.

"Hello?" The voice was pathetic, I thought. I wanted her to be stronger, and insist that we ship her kid back to Memphis. Family is what was needed here.

Gretchen introduced herself to Mariah's mother. I introduced myself, and did my usual nervous thing: I started talking quickly before I chickened out and clammed up, which was my other usual thing when uncomfortable. Not knowing how much the mom communicated with Ken, I knew I had to continue to tow the party line. "You don't know me, but I live on Isle au Haut. Your daughter is staying with me temporarily because Ken is in bad shape right now. He's abusing alcohol and is getting some help." This was about the nicest way I could tell the woman that she had mistakenly given her kid to an abusive drunk.

"Oh God!" That was stronger than the initial greeting, and I breathed a relieved sigh. "I have a sinus infection. I didn't need to hear *that* today. She can't come back here!"

Holy shit, I thought. Had I heard that correctly? Looking around the table at the looks of horror, I guessed that I had. I guess our conversation dribbled on from there. I suppose I said good-bye to the mom and hung up. But thinking back on it now, all I remember is being dumbfounded and shaking my head in disbelief while my friends did the same. I found a box of Kleenex and passed it around the table like a plate of cookies. I couldn't wait for everyone to leave my house so that I could call my own mother and confirm what I knew as normal maternal behavior.

The women did leave as soon as they could all pull themselves together. We all shared tight hugs—the kind you give and receive when someone has died and you can't seem to release the warm embrace. Each woman thanked me with great sincerity for taking care of Mariah while this mess got straightened out. No one wanted to think about foster care for a fifteen-year-old girl. That would probably not result in a happy ending.

After they left, I felt a closeness to this group of women that I had never experienced before. With the obvious exception of family, my friends, mentors, and support had always been male. Sure, I loved Brenda and Bill, and Kate had become a great friend, but sort of in a comradely way, like my male buddies. With Kate, rather than talking fishing, we talked food. There seemed something quite natural and very right about gaining female friends now. Until this time I had never noticed the unique power and strength in female bonds. I love my mother and sisters. But I had not ever had any real fondness for women other than family, nor had I ever had what I would refer to as a *real* female friend. I never wanted any. I knew that I had several now. These were not new, budding relationships that needed nurturing. These friendships were tight and immediate and as heartfelt as any I had with my longtime guy friends. Circumstances had plunged us into an unexpected and sudden intimacy, and it actually felt great.

The next few days were strange and strained. We waited not so patiently for some form of law enforcement to come and take Ken off our island. Brenda and my cousin, Dianne, had become the point people for all phone conversation and relaying of information in all directions. The truth of the situation was slowly but surely seeping from cracks and wicking to different nooks and crannies. Nothing was said directly to me. But I could tell that more and more community members were in the loop by their reactions to Mariah and me. The state police were eventually coming out to arrest Ken, but they hadn't told us when. Mariah continued to go to school, returning every afternoon and asking, "When are they coming?" Our county sheriff was so thoughtful, and worked hard to get answers to all persistent inquiries. The social worker from the Department of Health and Human Services, who called to check in daily, asked if I needed any money to help with the feeding and caring of Mariah, which I did not. The wheels were turning, just not quickly enough from an extremely anxious perspective.

I had not laid eyes on Ken since Mariah and I had gone to see Lesley six weeks before, which was fine by me. By all accounts, he was keeping to himself, only going out to the post office and off island to his agreed-upon therapy or counseling. Everyone was aware that he was not to see Mariah without her consent, which she was in no way willing to give even though he did make daily requests to me by e-mail, all very cordial. Our e-mail correspondence was civil, considering what I knew and assuming that he felt I was standing in the way of what he wanted. Ken was far from stupid. And he knew enough not to push too hard. He was acting in exactly the way I would have expected him to, considering what he knew of his own vulnerability if the truth were known, but he remained unaware that it was.

I was taking one day at a time, as recommended by a good

bumper sticker, and wondering what would eventually become of Mariah. I knew that wherever she ended up would be a huge improvement over where she'd been. People were treating me like some kind of hero for taking her in, which was embarrassing because I'd been looking forward to her exit from my house and life. Mariah spoke fondly of an aunt and uncle in Tennessee with whom she had lived from time to time before coming to Maine. They sounded like decent folks who had really cared for her. I assumed Mariah would end up with them. She also spoke often and lovingly of her grandmother. Mariah was proud to show me a photograph of this grandmother. Friends are great, but nothing compares to your own family. Returning to her true home, Memphis, would work out best for everyone in the long run, I thought.

My sister Bif was the only one with whom I could be honest about how I was really feeling—which was put upon; I was no self-sacrificing angel to my sister. I complained that Mariah was hard to have around. She just wanted to watch TV all of her waking hours, which were honestly too few for me to complain about. I didn't like having to lock my doors and have a loaded gun handy. Shouldn't Mariah be staying with someone who had a man in the house? And she was so sad, she'd put me in a major funk. And I was very uncomfortable knowing all that I did about how she had been abused. Bif always listened and never judged, although I am sure she should have.

Simon had just come to the island after having been home in Vermont, and he was at my place having a late lunch. We were basically catching up on my present unhappily not-alone status when the phone rang. It was the mail boat captain. He was calling to let me know that Ken was on the dock and waiting for the late boat for a ride home. Exasperated, I recalled that this was the day Ken had alcohol counseling, and of course that required a boat trip. But in the past he had taken his own boat, avoiding the mail boat for whatever reason. So until this second I hadn't worried that he might try to see Mariah. I knew that Mariah would be arriving from school at the dock in about thirty minutes. I thanked the captain for the heads-up and sprang into action. Simon's boat was faster than mine, so I recruited him for a ride to the mail boat dock in Stonington to intercept any chance (or not) meeting. It was the longest seven miles of my life. My heart was racing and I prayed that we would beat the school bus and head Mariah off before she might be forced to face Ken. I was frantic. The one thing I was supposed to do was to ensure that Mariah and Ken did not see each other until she was ready—and that was going to be never. Jesus! If I didn't get there in time, she'd be a basket case tonight, I thought. I begged Simon to push the throttle up. He assured me that *Scalawag* was doing all she could.

We arrived at the mail boat landing and I hit the dock running before Simon had a single line ashore. Thankfully, the bus was not yet in sight. But Ken was. I approached him quickly. "Ken! You know you aren't supposed to ride this boat without letting me know. You agreed!"

"Oh, sorry, Linda." He flicked his cigarette butt into the ocean. "I was just off having a counseling session, and I guess I forgot the rules." He rolled his eyes to emphasize his feelings. "But really, the crisis is over. It's time for Mariah to come home. She can't live with you forever."

Absolutely repulsed by his casual, cavalier attitude, I felt every part of me tense up. I gritted my teeth. I took a deep breath and said, "She can. And she will. We have always been up front with each other, so I want you to hear this from me. I am going to become Mariah's legal guardian. If you choose to fight me on this, you will lose."

CHAPTER 7

A Little Family

Whoa. Imagine my surprise to hear that from me. I might have been more shocked than Ken was. And yet, though it went directly against everything I had been saying and thinking, at least internally, it also felt right. Ken took two steps back because I was literally in his face. "I'm not ready for that to happen; maybe I never will be. Mariah is the only family I have. I just want her to come home," he said rather pathetically. His clothes, which were noticeably grungy, stood out now only because most island residents have an off-island wardrobe we save for trips to the mainland. I couldn't believe that Ken and I were the same age. He looked old and worn in his down-and-out drunk slump. His face was thin and hung sadly from his forehead, which was fully exposed in a bit of breeze that swept greasy tendrils of hair to his temples. He placed a hand over a silk-screened Jerry Garcia on the chest of his T-shirt and tapped his heart as if consoling it tenderly. The same hand reached for the breast pocket and flipped out a cigarette that magically landed in his mouth, lit in what seemed a fraction of a second.

On the very edge of my visual field, I saw Simon whisking Mariah behind and by Ken. They exited my peripheral border stage right and headed toward *Scalawag*. The image of a suspect with head draped in a coat to hide identity from a camera flashed in my mind. I didn't have another syllable to share with Ken. I repeated what I had already said, just to make it clear, and added that if he really cared about Mariah's well-being, he would sign off on the guardianship and allow the switch to be seamless. He said that it was a big decision and one that he wasn't emotionally healthy enough to make at this time. He acknowledged that he understood that should he resist, he would certainly lose. I then did what any good American would do and said, "You'll be hearing from my attorney." I turned from him and walked calmly and purposely to *Scalawag*, which bobbed slightly at the end of the wharf while I wondered why I didn't have an attorney.

Scalawag's engines purred happily while the external outdrives sputtered, burped, and whizzed strong saltwater streams. I threw the lines and stepped aboard while Simon maneuvered away from the dock and zigzagged through the lobster boats that rested on moorings after long, hard days of honest work. I stood in the stern and looked over the bow at Isle au Haut, which loomed above the smaller, lower islands that studded the sides of our path. Simon stood at the helm with Mariah beside him. I had better inform her now what my intentions are, I thought. Ultimately it would be her decision, not mine. But until now I was sure she hadn't anything to contemplate, just fears that are cultivated by the unknown. It was time to thumb-up the eyelid.

I don't typically hem and haw or tiptoe around awkward conversation topics. I dive in headfirst and worry about the depth of water in midair. I moved to Mariah's left and joined her in holding the dash for balance as the boat sped along toward home. "Sorry the bus-to-boat transition was so dramatic," I offered with a smile.

"It's okay." Mariah's eyes focused on something over the bow. There was a short pause, and then she asked, "Why were you talking to him?" She was nervous, nearly accusatory.

"I was informing him that I am going to become your legal guardian." I was looking directly at Mariah, who had no physical reaction to the grenade I had just tossed other than a narrowing of her eyes. I felt Simon tense up. Awkward doesn't come close to describing how I felt in the silence that followed. I stared at Mariah and Simon, both of whom stared straight ahead, seemingly preferring nothingness to eye contact with me. I sighed in a bit of relief after unloading. I knew it was unfair of me to expect any verbal reaction from Mariah right now. She needed time to digest what I hadn't taken time to chew. "Of course," I continued, "it is entirely up to you."

"Okay." Okay? The one word was toneless. There was no indication of emotion in any direction. Okay that I had spoken to Ken? Okay that I wanted to become her guardian? Okay that it was her choice? Not that I was expecting joy or a three-way hug, but this other extreme forced a tear to pool up in the corner of my eye that threatened to roll down my cheek should I blink, which I did not. I do not cry often, never have. But when I do, it's a good one that might last for days. I wouldn't waste a tear or two now. This wasn't worth it. So I swallowed hard, shrugged, and became the third of the "no evil" monkeys, suddenly fascinated with the view over the bow.

It seemed a strange form of stare-down contest, which struck me as funny (although I didn't laugh; hell, I didn't even consider a half grin). Whoever broke the trance first lost. We were more than halfway home. I could gaze empty-eyed with my mind brimming over forever. My thoughts were focused, but I might as well have been totally blind for all that registered in the line of sight. Focused thoughts did not mean organized or clear, just not wandering. I wondered what I had just gotten into with the suggestion that I would take on a teenage girl—and an abused kid at that! I had no idea what Mariah had been through beyond what she had shared so far. But my gut said that there was more to the story.

Yes, I had wanted children. But would I be in over my head beginning with this one? Mariah had been a challenge even at the safe distance I had maintained with her status as temporary houseguest, and I'd been counting the days till she moved out. Making this arrangement legal and permanent was probably a bad idea, I thought. And now it was too late. I had opened my big mouth. There was always a chance that Mariah would not want me to become her guardian. But what other options did she have? Foster care? Would life with me be her consolation prize?

I wished I could turn back the clock to just one hour ago. One hour ago I was eagerly waiting to be set free from the burden of responsibility for this girl. I had shot my mouth off first to Ken and then, more important, to Mariah. There was no way I could take it back now. It had to have come from somewhere real inside me, but what did it really mean? Guardianship and all things maternal fit neatly into the category of things about which I am clueless.

Suddenly there was a terrible noise that came from the stern of the boat, and we slowed down dramatically enough to send us all into a lurch toward the forward bulkhead, which we braced ourselves against. I knew immediately that one or both of the propellers had become tangled by pot warp, the line that runs from a lobster trap to the buoy on the surface. Thanks, God, I thought—something I know how to deal with! I told Simon to pull both throttles back to dead idle and knock both engines out of gear while I hustled to the stern and climbed over the transom and onto the swim platform, where I could see a line trailing behind from the starboard propeller. I instructed Simon to shut down the starboard engine and raise the outdrive, bringing the fouled propeller to the surface. Mariah, who had seen this drill a few times aboard the *Mattie Belle* during the season she had worked for me, grabbed Simon's boat hook (on a fishing boat it's called a gaff) and handed it to me. I hooked the line and yanked, but it was too tight for me to pull it to where I could wind it off the propeller. I asked Simon to back down (place the port engine in reverse) so that I could gain some slack with which to work. He did, and I did. The line was clear, and a few seconds later a buoy shot out from under the boat like a missile. Simon lowered the starboard outdrive, restarted the engine, and off we went toward home.

"Thanks, Linny," Simon called over his shoulder as I sat on the bench seat that straddled the stern.

"No problem," I answered with a slight wave, wishing that I had no problem. Thirty years of boats and fishing had fine-tuned problem solving of the salty nature. There wasn't a situation at sea that I wasn't confident I could remedy. I had made every conceivable mistake that could be made (at least once) and thus had firsthand experience in getting back on track. But this present situation involved emotions and people not in my repertoire. I could fix anything mechanical, weather any storm, persist and endure through poor fishing and low morale, but none of that practical stuff mattered today. The seaworthiness I had always aspired to meant very little now.

The tide was dead low, requiring that Simon pull back both throttles to idle in order to navigate "the ditch." As we snaked through the narrow thoroughfare between Isle au Haut and Kimball Island, Mariah joined me on the bench seat. She looked at me, I think for the first time since we had met. She didn't look around me, through me, or over my head. She really looked at me. "How do we do it?" she asked.

This was no time for dramatics or for dodges. I answered honestly. "I have no idea. But I will find out. And if it's something that you want to happen, it will happen." She nodded and jumped up to grab the stern line in time to take a couple of wraps around a piling at the town dock. "I'll help Simon put the boat on the mooring. You can wait in the truck or walk home and I'll meet you there," I said, knowing full well that she would not walk.

As Simon pulled the boat up to the dinghy that was tethered to his mooring, I made my way to the bow with the boat hook. I reached down, gaffed the dinghy's painter, pulled the mooring's spliced loop out of the water, and placed it over the cleat, securing it with a couple of hitches of smaller line. I untied the dinghy and walked it back around the house and to the transom, where we could easily climb in. While Simon shut down the boat, I sat in the stern of the dinghy, holding the side of *Scalawag* so that Simon could step right into the middle seat and row us ashore. He placed oars in locks and started pulling smoothly and rhythmically. The beat of the sound of the oars against locks, then water, then air lulled me soothingly, as the sound of good rowing always does. "I hope you know what you are getting yourself into," Simon advised. "Mariah may be beyond saving. You have no idea what demons she'll be fighting or for how long."

"She needs me," I said. "And I need her. I have lived a very selfish life so far. I need to be responsible for someone other than myself for a change."

"But legal guardianship? Do you really want to take that on? You know I am always here for you in moral support, but I would never be part of any binding legal paperwork."

"Who asked you to?" Even I was surprised by my swift response. This was the only instance in the eight years of our best-friend-and-companion relationship that I had felt truly disconcerted. Yes, the truth was that I had been squirming to terminate any real involvement with Simon beyond a round of golf or a day on the slopes for nearly a year now. But since Mariah had moved in with me, I had had second thoughts. So perhaps what I felt was not for Simon but for me. Whether it was adult company or a sympathetic ear or just plain help with jobs around the house and a boat that takes two people, I had allowed us to slip back into what I had struggled emotionally to be done with. While I appreciated Simon's honesty, the reality was that he would not "be there" for me or Mariah. I just knew from my experience with him that when the going gets tough, Simon disappears. He just does not deal well with drama. And I suppose that my independence and general low maintenance and lack of neediness had been part of my appeal. While I battled my own second thoughts and dreads, I didn't need any negative input from him. I was capable of providing that all by myself. Now that I was sure that I had injured Simon's feelings, and being extremely nonconfrontational, I asked, "Want to have dinner with us? I won't make you sign anything tonight."

Before dinner I walked down to my parents' house, knowing that I had better bring them into the loop before someone else did. Their reaction to the news that I was pursuing guardianship of Mariah was predictable. My mother and father, being good parents, were compelled to protect me. I have often felt like the slightly retarded daughter when my mother warns me about being taken advantage of. It wasn't all that long ago, I recalled, that my mother had advised me to "look in the mirror and practice saying no." So it was no surprise when my folks shared their opinion that I could be making a huge mistake and that there might be nothing I could do for Mariah beyond what I had al-

ready done. "Linny, you have no idea what that girl has been
through. She needs professional help. You're not equipped to deal
with this." After assuring Mom and Dad that I did indeed have
a clue as to what I was undertaking, that it was too late to back
out, and that I *wanted* to assume guardianship, they did reluctantly agree to support my decision even though they believed it
was a bad one.

So the next day I started researching the how-to part of legal
guardianship. I Googled and made phone calls until my brain
was saturated. Adoption seemed absurd because Mariah was already fifteen. I found a female attorney in Portland who specialized in family law and made an appointment. I don't know who
was more nervous going into the meeting, Mariah or me. We sat
silently in the stark waiting room at Pine Tree Legal Services.
Although there was nothing left of her nails to bite, Mariah
chewed the ends of her fingers relentlessly and jiggled her legs up
and down, bouncing on the balls of her feet rapidly. When the
end table began to vibrate, rattling the lamp it held, I placed a
hand on Mariah's knee and said, "Stop. You're driving me nuts."

"Sorry. I can't help it. Why are we here so early?" Mariah
looked at her cell phone. "Our appointment isn't for another ten
minutes!"

"Sorry. *I* can't help it. I am a chronic early bird."

"Geez. I could have slept another hour."

"I didn't sleep last night."

"Neither did I. Can we get something to eat when we get out
of here?" The base of the lamp continued to keep the beat to
Mariah's drumming and was accompanied by an occasional loud

sigh signifying that impatience was joining her nerves. She gnawed her cuticles relentlessly.

"Yup. You seem to be hungry," I said with a degree of sarcasm that didn't stop the nail biting. I sat stock-still, arms crossed at my chest as I bit my lower lip. My lips were slightly chapped and rather than search for my ChapStick, I occupied the waiting time chewing tiny pieces of skin from them until I managed to draw blood.

Mariah handed me a Kleenex and said, "You must be hungry, too." I couldn't help but smile, and acknowledging the nerves seemed to sooth them. I wasn't sure what was causing the conspicuous disquiet in Mariah, but imagined it could have been the possibility of having to repeat her embarrassing past yet again to a stranger. On the other hand, I was acutely aware of why I was anxious: I was taking another step toward something I was so unsure about, that I had no confidence. If the guardianship turned out badly, there would sure be a lot of people who could claim to have told me so.

Our meeting was somewhat impersonal and quick, much to our shared relief. Mariah and I learned together at this first and only meeting with the attorney that it was Mariah whom she would represent in the guardianship case (I would have to get my own lawyer, and did). The law required that the ward petition the court for a change in guardianship. When questioned by the attorney, Mariah looked at me for the answer, as if seeking assurance. I assumed that I should not lead Mariah in any direction, so I just nodded each time she looked at me. I certainly didn't want this to appear to have been *all* my idea just because it was.

Finally, the attorney began spoon-feeding Mariah by making each inquiry a simple yes or no question. Did Mariah agree that a change in guardianship was necessary? Yes. Did Mariah want to terminate her ward status with Ken? Yes. Did Mariah understand that she could nominate a new guardian for consideration? Yes. Did Mariah want to nominate Linda Greenlaw for her guardianship? Yes. And that was the first and only indication from Mariah that she wanted to go through with my suggestion. I tried not to listen to my own conscience telling me that Mariah had no other option.

Maybe it wasn't quite as simple as I remember it. But that is honestly what I recall. I don't remember any conversation about what had happened with Ken or her biological mother, or about any of the other traumatic events of her childhood leading up to our appearance together in that room, or anything actually personal. I've heard of more complicated arrangements to adopt a dog from a shelter. The attorney explained what would come next. Paperwork would be filled out and filed with the state, and a copy would be mailed to Ken asking that he sign away his legal responsibility and return the signed document to the attorney within two weeks. If he refused, then steps would be taken to force him to give up his charge. So the ball was in motion and soon to be on Ken's side of the net. The attorney also explained that Mariah's biological mother would also have to sign a document, as she had when Ken took charge of her daughter, relinquishing any parental control or responsibility. Eventually, and whether Ken and the mother signed off—willingly or not—our case would go before a judge and guardianship would probably be granted. The attorney would handle all of this, and free of charge because she was representing a minor. Mariah and I both shook the attorney's hand, thanked her, and left the building feeling a little lighter. We climbed into opposite sides of the Jeep, slammed doors simultaneously, clicked seat belts, and exhaled in perfect harmony. "Can we eat? I'm starving," Mariah said.

"Me, too. What do you feel like?" Of course I meant this only in reference to what she might like to have for lunch, and not at all metaphysically. The last thing I wanted to do right now was probe inside either of our brains or souls.

The following week was agonizing. Because the accusations made against Ken involved child pornography and crossing state lines, the charges, when and if they were ever in place, would be federal. The result of this seemed to be that more time was needed. The extenuating circumstance seemed to be that we live on an island. Logistically this was somewhat new territory for the agencies involved. We waited to hear when Ken would be arrested, and hoped that he would sign off on guardianship before that happened. It's hard to believe that Ken wandered around as free as a bird during this period or, in his case, as free as a caged bird because he'd chosen to remain a hermit. I was feeling a lot of things; on the top of the list was helplessness. I continued to lock my house every night. I lived with a knot in my gut that squeezed bitterness into my throat perpetually. The phone calls and morning meetings for coffee at my kitchen table were ongoing. Everyone, whether fully in the loop or just partially, wanted to be up to speed on what was happening, and everyone had fingers crossed that things would go as well as they could. I had daily calls from island women lending support, both emotional and physical. I received cards and notes and e-mail from people who wanted to help me do the right thing with respect to this new relationship. The offers were refreshing and much appreciated. Mariah went off to school every day on the boat, and we were fed dinner by friends and neighbors any night we accepted an invitation. Some friends called just to say they were thinking of us and were willing and available to do anything to help.

Simon was in and out between Vermont and the island, and fulfilled his role of providing moral support well. We were back to "normal," and I appreciated his friendship now more than ever. The timing was bad for any other significant change in our lives, Mariah's or mine. When he was around, he and Mariah clicked. She joked with him about recent events in the news, or at least the happenings that she found noteworthy. Because she got such a kick out of Simon's ignorance of tabloid news, Simon began doing his homework and questioning her about Brad and J Lo and whatever rapper had beaten his girlfriend. By the same token, Mariah had to bone up on current events less interesting to her by watching CNN and Fox News. We watched *Jeopardy* every night before dinner and with the three of us working as a team, we didn't miss many. Weirdly, I started thinking of us as a little family, so I put more effort into meals than I otherwise would have just for me. Even though this was a nervous and miserable time in my life, I felt very much a part of the island community in that everyone shared equally in the misery and waiting. I felt united with Simon and Mariah. At no point did I ever feel alone.

Mariah now greeted me with the same two questions every

day after she slammed the door of the truck. "Did he sign?" and "When are they coming?" My cousin, Dianne, is responsible for carrying the mail between the post office and the mail boat. Although I am sure it is not legal to riffle through the mail bag to look for a certain Priority Mail envelope addressed to a certain attorney in Portland, she somehow managed to give me a thumbs-down every morning when I dropped Mariah at the boat. I was very worried that Ken would not sign. And if he hadn't signed by the time he was arrested, there was a big, terrifying question mark regarding where Mariah would end up. Ken and I engaged in a short e-mail correspondence in which I encouraged him to resign guardianship because it would be the best thing for Mariah. And we all wanted what was best for her. Ken dragged his feet. He just couldn't do it yet, he said. I also worried that he would dump all incriminating evidence into the ocean before it could be confis-cated. Although we had done well about keeping tight-lipped, Ken would eventually figure out that Mariah had probably told us, or the social worker, about what really had gone on in their house. I worried that in his unstable state, he might come unglued and attempt bodily harm to himself, or worse, Mariah. The calls from the Department of Health and Human Services continued, mostly from Gretchen, the social worker assigned to our case. She always asked if I *needed* anything. No, I didn't need money or professional help with coping. Or at least I didn't think so.

We were closing in on the two-week deadline for Ken's resig-nation of guardianship. I got word from the county sheriff that two state police officers and a special federal agent were coming to the island the next day. They couldn't ride the mail boat, so they would be brought out from Rockland, which is clear across Penobscot Bay, by the U.S. Coast Guard. I was asked to meet the Coast Guard boat offshore with my boat and lead them to our town dock. From there our first selectman would transport the officials to Ken's house. Of course I agreed, more than ready for this long-awaited juncture. The county sheriff would accompany me aboard my vessel as would the first selectman. A time and rendezvous point was set. The handful of islanders who were aware of the pending arrest spent several nerve-racking hours surmising and worrying on the telephone. I didn't sleep that night.

I dropped Mariah off at the boat and was thrilled to get a thumbs-up from the mail-carrying cousin. Okay, I thought, one down, one to go. Soon after the mail boat pulled away and headed ashore, the county sheriff arrived in his own boat, ready to make a trip offshore with me. The first selectman was promptly at the dock just as I brought the *Mattie Belle* in from the mooring. The men stepped aboard and off we went.

Fortunately, it was a brilliantly clear day. The breeze was fickle, flirting with the sun, and yet embracing as it delivered a chill it held from caressing the bay. It was the kind of day that lets you know winter is on its way, but when I turned the boat just right, the sun's blaze on the ocean connived to suggest that autumn was in no particular hurry to yield to the next season. We passed the lighthouse at Robinson Point and I felt good that I was now *doing* something. I liked the feeling of the cold wheel in my hands. My confidence soared. The knot in my stomach melted away as I steered for a position off Kimball Head, where I could see the entrance to Fox Island Thoroughfare from where the Coast Guard boat would be coming. This is what I understood. This was my comfort zone. This was the day we had all been waiting for, and I was happy to be a spoke in the wheel of justice that seemed to finally be spinning.

I knocked the engine out of gear. We drifted, rolling gently from crest to trough to crest of swells that displayed nothing but blue. The sheriff looked at his wristwatch, then at me. I raised my eyebrows and shoulders in unison. He said, "It's time." The agreed-upon time of rendezvous was ten o'clock. I scoured the horizon to our west, trying to pick a boat out of the shoreline. I saw nothing. "Probably just running a little late," the sheriff said. I found it strange that the Coast Guard would be late to arrive at a point and time they themselves had set. Didn't they have the best state-of-the-art electronic equipment for navigation? They have stuff that civilian mariners don't yet have access to. And aren't they heavily trained and highly skilled? Weird that they couldn't figure out an ETA accurately, I thought. But realizing that I might be a bit uptight about what might transpire and perhaps unfairly impatient, I forced myself to sit on the gunwale rather than stand at attention at the helm.

Sitting patiently didn't last long. I grabbed a pair of binoculars and searched again. I saw nothing. "Maybe I should call them on the radio," I suggested. Both men agreed that a call was in order because the CG was now officially forty minutes late. After two attempts, I received an answer from the very apologetic Coast Guard. They had experienced traffic coming out of Rockland. Just so you nonboating people know, that was the most ridiculous thing I had ever heard. Traffic? In Rockland Harbor? That time of year? But you are the U.S. Coast Guard, I thought. Maybe they experienced heavy traffic on Route 1 on their way to the CG station, I hoped. The nice voice on the radio confirmed that they would be exiting Fox Island Thoroughfare in five minutes. I thanked the man, and felt a huge sense of relief. Now all I had to do was wait for them to come near, and lead them to the dock. Phew.

Well, five minutes turned into fifteen. I finally spied the CG boat coming out of the notch on the horizon that I know as Fox Island. With the binoculars I could see the telltale red stripe against the white hull. "Here they come." I smiled. And as I watched the boat turn to the south and increase speed, I said "And there they go." The boat was approximately ninety degrees off course. "Where the hell are they going?"

"Matinicus?" offered the sheriff, mentioning the only island or land mass the CG might find south of us before hitting Cape Cod. "Head them off." And I tried. But they were too far away and moving much faster than the *Mattie Belle* could manage. I really didn't want to be on the radio any more than necessary as I was still thinking that this was to be a somewhat covert operation. There was a long-standing stereotype among the members of the commercial fishing world that all Coasties were from Kansas, or some other landlocked home, but it didn't seem that funny right now. We chased the boat for a while hoping someone aboard might happen to see us and mention to the captain or navigator that they were being pursued. But it was no use. They were putting quite a distance between us. I had no other choice than to radio them again.

I asked the very nice and youthful voice to please come to port about ninety degrees. And lo and behold, we watched the boat, which was now no bigger than a dot, grow to what once again resembled a Coast Guard vessel. When it was clear that they had no idea which boat on the ocean I was aboard, even after I gave them my position in latitude and longitude, I asked the nice boy to stop where he was. "Just knock your vessel out of gear, and I will come to you. Please. Over." Once I was close enough to ensure there was no mistaking the *Mattie Belle* for any other boat, I waved an arm at the CG boat and motioned them to follow me. They responded by waving in the other direction, beckoning me to come closer, which I did. I got right up alongside their vessel so that I could communicate without the radio.

There were three uniformed men on the deck of the boat, all dressed in navy blue and sporting orange life vests. The door on the upper deck of the bridge opened and another uniformed man stepped out. They all looked like kids, which I sadly realized was more an indication of my age than theirs. The officer above informed me that he was unauthorized to take his vessel to the dock as the depth of water on the navigational chart was insufficient for the draft of the boat of which he was in command. I asked what she drew, and he replied that he needed ten feet of water in order to get permission to proceed. "It doesn't look like you draw ten feet," I commented. He agreed that the boat did not need that much water, but the rules governing what he could do did. "Well, there's at least ten feet there now. You'll be all set." He apologized and explained that things weren't that simple. He did not have permission from someone who was calling the shots from ashore, and could not, under any circumstances, proceed any farther. He then suggested that I secure my boat to his and transfer the three people he had transported to this point. This was dumbfounding. And not at all what I wanted. This part of the bargain was unnecessary. There was plenty of water at the dock. We had waited so long for this day. I deduced that I would also be transporting the officers along with Ken back to the Coast Guard boat. I was nervous about Ken. Did I really want to face him in this situation? No, I did not. But what other option did I have?

I made a circle and lined up to secure my starboard side to the CG vessel's port side. So far this mission qualified as keystone cop material. My confidence in the result was flagging. Although the weather was fair, the sea was far from calm. The swells rolled the Coast Guard boat nearly rail to rail because she was fairly round bottomed. The CG crew scrambled to secure large fenders to their port side where I could hopefully make a landing long enough for the police officers to jump ship. I stuck the landing and handed one of the crew members a short line to cleat off while the sheriff did the same at the stern.

Three people emerged from within the CG vessel and stepped somewhat athletically from bouncing boat to bouncing boat. The first thing that struck me was the physical appearance of the three officers. Two very fit and handsome men, and one extremely fit and gorgeous woman thanked me for coming out to get them. They could have stepped right off a movie set—they so looked the part of the good guys. The CG crew released my lines, and off we went. My three new passengers introduced themselves— all special agents, two with the state police and one with the FBI.

So, I gathered, this was the A team. And as we steamed toward the dock, the conversation restored all of my confidence. I was impressed. Scared, but really impressed.

What scared me most was the new knowledge that this team had neither a warrant for Ken's arrest nor a search warrant. They had experience with similar situations but, it seemed, nothing else. Something about their presence—demeanor or professionalism—prohibited me from asking the logical question: "So what the hell are we doing today?" They obviously knew what they were doing, which was quite comforting. But I was absolutely sick with worry now that I would be transporting this special team back to the Coast Guard vessel without Ken. Then what? Forcing that dark thought back into the depths from where it came, I eased the *Mattie Belle* into the float at our town landing, relieved to have no witnesses. All passengers except the sheriff, who stayed with me, disembarked, asking that I remain at the float until they returned for their ride back offshore. I don't know which was stronger, wanting to be the proverbial fly on the wall at Ken's house or the repulsion of knowing what had happened over the course of years that had led to today and wanting to hide under a rock until it was over. I could do neither. So I had nothing to do but sit aboard the *Mattie Belle* with the sheriff and wait.

"Isn't that the mail boat coming?" the sheriff asked.

Sure enough, the *Mink* was approaching the float with a deck loaded with lumber and other building supplies. All freight coming to Isle au Haut does so across the end of the town landing, where I was now tied. I would need to move to make room for the *Mink* to secure directly under the hydraulic winch so that the freight could be off-loaded. I heard a truck backing down the dock, coming to receive the supplies. Poor timing, I thought, as I started the engine, dropped lines, and idled out of the way. Judging from the size of their load, the *Mink* would be here awhile, I thought. "I guess we might as well hang on my mooring," I said as I moved in that direction. This was just another wrinkle in the fiasco.

Secured to the mooring, the sheriff and I sat on the engine box of the *Mattie Belle,* where we were sheltered from the cool breeze and fully exposed to the sun. We watched as bundles of cedar shingles and stacks of lumber were lifted from the deck of the *Mink,* swung dangling from the end of the boom, and lowered onto the back of the flatbed truck. Over and over, up and down—it was like clowns climbing out of the tiny circus car. How much freight could the boat possibly carry? My heart skipped a beat when I saw the selectman's red Jeep Cherokee come tearing down the ramp and onto the wharf.

The sheriff and I both jumped to our feet. We watched as the selectman climbed out of the driver's side of the Jeep. The other doors remained closed. Although I peered with all my might, the glare on the Jeep's windshield didn't allow my nervous stare to penetrate. The selectman stepped aboard the *Mink* and disappeared into the cabin. The selectman called me from the *Mink*'s radio. When I answered, he said, "They asked him some pointed questions, to which he confessed. Then he faked a seizure. We are now waiting for him to be cleared medically before they can proceed." I had no idea to what Ken had confessed, nor did I understand how he might get medical clearance or how the officials would proceed. In spite of all of my ignorance, I thanked the selectman for letting me know. I understood that I was to be on standby for something at some time. And that was it.

I cast off the mooring and steamed to the dock where the selectman was just about to climb into his Jeep. I needed more information and wasn't going to get it over the radio. He saw me coming and surely sensed my bewilderment. I threw the *Mattie Belle* into reverse just long and hard enough to come to a complete stop just astern of the mail boat. He came to the edge of the dock where I was close enough to converse at low volume. He knelt down to get as close as he could and said, "He volunteered enough information for a judge to issue a search warrant and a warrant for his arrest over the phone. I'm not sure how much longer it will be, but they are not leaving the island without him."

I was greatly relieved to hear of the impending arrest. But I was very unhappy with the thought of being part of whatever would happen from here. "Thanks. That's good news. I'm not having him aboard my boat. The Coast Guard will have to come get him," I said bluntly. I promptly picked up the radio and called the Coast Guard vessel that was still waiting offshore. I knew that they had heard about the seizure, and assumed they'd had phone contact to know what I had just learned of the arrest. "I don't think it's prudent or safe to do an at-sea transfer of this guy who is having seizures. If fact, I don't think I can be held responsible for getting him to you safely. You'll have to come to the dock and pick him up. There's plenty of water here now, and the tide is rising." I was asked to stand by, which I did while assuming the young officer was now in contact with his superiors. The answer came back asking that I come out to get one of the officers from the boat, show him the way to the dock, show him the depth of water, and then, if the officer agreed that it was safe to proceed to the dock, I could come back for them and they would follow close behind.

I was so anxious and stressed out, I steamed at full throttle to pick up the officer, who jumped before I was secured to the vessel. I steamed the distance to the dock, talking the entire time about the channel, what to avoid, and which side of the day marker to be on coming and going. I pointed at my depth sounder continually, commenting on the deep water we had everywhere. I prayed for a mark of ten feet at the dock, and was relieved to see twelve. "See? There's plenty of water here, and this is the shoalest point." The kid was young and inexperienced. I could tell he trusted me but didn't want to be responsible for making a bad decision. "And I'll lead the way. There's no way to get in any trouble," I pleaded. The sheriff chimed in to support my argument. He added that the Coast Guard should not expect a civilian to transport what was now a suspect under arrest, especially when it was so unnecessary.

We zipped back to the Coast Guard boat, allowed the young officer to hop off the *Mattie Belle*, and headed for the dock for what I hoped would be the final trip of the day. The Coast Guard followed close behind, breaking away when I turned for my mooring. I watched as they tied to the town landing in the berth that the mail boat had now vacated. As I shut electronics and engine down, I couldn't help but have an overwhelming sense of doom. Nothing had gone right today. Was this an omen of some kind telling me that I was making a mistake? It was not a good feeling, and one that I tried desperately to persuade to subside. What if Simon and my parents had been right? The sense of impending doom at the hands of a decision I had made against the advice of the three most relied upon people in my life had the effect of making me feel very weak and small, quite the opposite of what I needed to feel. It wasn't as if I could say "so far, so good" with regard to my relationship with Mariah. In fact, it was strained at best. I had never been more truthful than when I told Simon that I had lived very selfishly to this point in my life. And now I was making a major commitment to share when I had been unwilling to do so with anyone to date. I had made bad decisions before and lived with them. But my mistakes in the past hadn't involved more than someone's paycheck—usually mine. You can always make more money. But how would you go about fixing screwed-up hopes and dreams and futures? I wanted to believe that I would be more than just the best of bad options for Mariah. I *had* to be more than the least of all evils. I was confused. What I knew for certain was that it would have been easier, a lot easier, to spend the rest of my life alone. But I also knew that easier did not always mean better.

If I was doing the right thing, why was I virtually hiding in the parking lot waiting for the red Jeep to reappear? Why was *I* feeling ashamed? All that I had done to this point had been so bold and brave. Why was I now cowardly and unable to face Ken?

I have spent many hours wondering what caused those feelings, and have never been able to justify or psychoanalyze to any satisfaction. But when the Jeep roared down the hill and onto the dock, I had to see and not be seen. I had to watch Ken helped out of the vehicle, unhandcuffed long enough to be helped into a survival suit and rehandcuffed and helped aboard the Coast Guard boat, where he disappeared into the cabin. I raced to my house, arriving in time to watch the Coast Guard boat go by and disappear behind Robinson Point. The kids from Kansas appeared to be off course by about ninety degrees. But Ken was gone, and since then not a day has passed that I haven't been very thankful for that.

CHAPTER 8

What's Another Cat?

O ut of sight, but not out of mind, Ken left behind more than a kid, as it turned out. I suppose it was my naïveté that held fast to the notion that all the badness and fear that had enveloped my small circle of friends and family who had endured the burden of the whole truth and kept it secret would be sucked down the drain with the dirty water as soon as the handcuffs snapped around Ken's wrists. It was perhaps idealism that wheedled my heavy mind-set to the lighter prospects of everything working out for the best now that the bad seed had been disinterred. To the contrary; the weeks that followed closely behind the arrest opened a gaping wound that bled freely from the island's heart and soul. The possibility of healing our community bore the same degree of remoteness that the chances of our having a practicing pedophile in our midst had done just a short, innocent while ago. The awareness that Ken had lived among *us* while living such a sleazy, filthy life left more than a scar.

Not the least of what Ken left behind was Cowgirl, the sickly, skinny, stinking cat. Because I am not a lover of all of God's little creatures, I resisted when asked to adopt Cowgirl. And that was before I had laid eyes on the ratty feline. To say that I had a weak moment would be quite an understatement. Weak? I was put under the barrage of the masses at my lowest point. I had been reduced to tears. I totally dissolved in front of the entire town of Isle au Haut. Oh, it wasn't the cat that I was publically bawling my eyes out about. Those tears didn't come until a little later. My public crying jag was a complete culmination of everything that Ken had left behind *but* the cat.

The idea of an informal town meeting designed to dispel any rumors and set straight any misinformation regarding Ken's removal from our island and Mariah's future here seemed logical. The Clarks and I agreed that now that Ken had been arrested and removed from our island, it would be safe and in fact prudent to be forthcoming with the information that we had kept quiet until this time. This was a chance to inform the entire community and begin the healing process. There was little chance that just about everyone had neither seen nor heard about the Coast Guard boat, special agents, and Ken's farewell in cuffs and immersion suit. So it was only fair to let the community in on the truth rather than let a few facts generate more rumors. Mariah's counselor, Lesley, graciously agreed at my request to attend the meeting to provide some statistics, her opinion of what would eventually happen with Ken legally, what Mariah might be experiencing emotionally, and how best for us all to cope with the various ways we might be affected. As a rule, islanders clutch their emotional cards particularly close. We are an emotional and passionate people, but outsiders looking in might feel more of a chill. I know the cliché holds that still waters run deep, but trust me, a blank stare from an islander is indicative of nothing. The surface can be dead calm while things roil within.

With Mariah safely at home on the couch, I chose this particular moment for a meltdown. I stood in front of the town of Isle au Haut (all forty-five of them) thinking it appropriate for me to introduce Lesley and explain why she was there. I didn't get far. I began to sob uncontrollably and had to sit down and allow someone else take over. While the story of Ken's abuse unfolded, I was joined in tears by many. To this day I recall Sue MacDonald weeping and saying, "Both of my girls have spent many nights at that house." I also recall the veins in her husband's neck pulsating noticeably as he stared at his feet. Dave Hiltz, also a dad of a young island girl, clenched his jaw and both fists as he listened, staring straight ahead. Yes, it was a good thing word hadn't gotten out prematurely. Ken would have been taken off in a body bag. By the end of the meeting everyone was frightfully in the know.

The questions eventually came around to logistics. What would eventually become of Ken, legally and practically? And in the meantime, what would happen with Ken's lobster traps and skiff? What about his pickup truck and VW Rabbit? What about the house he rented from the town, and could he be evicted? They might seem like petty details, but these were important issues in island life. Nobody had answers even to these more comfortable, less emotional queries. The town's lawyer would be consulted (right, we didn't have a cop, but we had a lawyer!). Everything had to be done by the book. And once we had a clear understanding of what the town's rights were, we assumed that the town would be responsible for cleaning out the house it had rented to Ken now that he had vacated it. I was invited to go through the house to collect whatever might be there in the way of paperwork needed for the pending guardianship, which I assumed would happen quickly and soon. Relieved that I had finally reached the bottom of the well of tears, I was minutes from a clean getaway when someone mentioned Cowgirl.

All fingers pointed at me. I should have the cat. The cat, everyone reasoned, was all Mariah loved in the world. Nobody else seemed to want the cat. That should have been a warning to me. Even people who themselves owned many cats didn't step up to the plate for Cowgirl. "What's one more cat?"—I never heard that from any of the cat people. Cats, to my mind, are innately sneaky, not just in their instinctive hunting and preying type of stealth, which I might otherwise admire, but in their deceit. What other animal hides its own poop? That little trick alone points to a degree of cunning that makes me leery. After making it abundantly clear to all that I was less than enthusiastic about the add-on, I reluctantly agreed to take the cat, expecting Mariah to care for it. I could buy the food. The rest would be up to her. And I thought that was absolutely appropriate as I recalled the same arrangement throughout my childhood of pets, both cats and dogs. I would make it work in spite of my qualms. I don't remember who volunteered to deliver Cowgirl to my house, and it's a good thing I don't. But as promised, the cat arrived at my place the next day, litter box and all.

The presence of Cowgirl did make Mariah smile. And I suppose that in and of itself eased the otherwise painful experience of Cowgirl as a housemate. But the smiles were fleeting. Mariah was genuinely unhappy, and she verbalized this unhappiness mostly about her school situation. The daily boat rides back and forth prevented Mariah from having school friends and activity outside of class. She had absolutely no social life beyond dinner with me (I happen to think that I am excellent company, but apparently I am not everyone's cup of tea). All of the island girls Mariah's age were off at boarding schools, so she had nobody to hang out with on weekends (other than me). At first, our home was a bit happier when Simon was around. But soon Mariah stopped putting on her nice face for him, and he experienced our more typical unpleasantness. Mariah and I had many short conversations that all began to sound alike. "Can't you make some friends who have kids my age?" Mariah asked pleadingly.

"Can't you make your own friends?" I asked.

"Right. And *where* would I find these potential friends?"

"Gee. Let me think . . . where would you find kids your age? I know! How about school?" I had learned some of this sarcasm from Mariah herself.

"At Stonington High School?" Mariah's tone now indicated that I had pissed her off by not agreeing to somehow cultivate new friendships with people who had teenage kids. And her opinion of her classmates was, I thought, unjustifiably low. How could

I have the audacity to suggest that she become chums with the likes of them? When I saw Mariah begin to withdraw into the couch cushions, I should have let it go. But sometimes it takes awhile for me to learn how best to handle certain emotional situations. I mean, Mariah hadn't exactly come with an owner's manual.

"No. Not Stonington. Are you kidding? I know! Let's place a personal ad for you. 'Teenage girl seeks teenage girls for friendship. Likes: Cats. Dislikes: Everything but cats. Interests: None. Residents of Stonington need not apply.' That ought to get some action." Now Mariah put a pillow over her head and I knew she was weeping. I learned the hard way that Mariah could dish, but she couldn't take. Whenever I got drawn into this immature banter, I was sure that I ended up feeling worse than she did. I sincerely wanted to be a good guardian, but she just seemed so ridiculous at times.

I was much more sympathetic toward Mariah's complaints about her education than I was toward her social life. Mariah was taking classes at Stonington that she had already had her freshman year at Evergreen. So "bored," "lame," "stupid," and "hate" made up the vast majority of Mariah's vocabulary. She wanted to go back to Evergreen as badly as I wanted it. Yes, it would be a better education for her. Yes, it would be a healthier social situation for her. Yes, she was making me miserable and I couldn't wait to get her out of the house. I promised Mariah to make it my sole mission in life.

Just as I was opening the lines of communication with the administration at Evergreen Academy, I became Mariah's legal guardian. It was a painless and almost scarily simple process. The paperwork was in order. We were met by Mariah's attorney in Rockland, where the county courthouse is. We sat before a judge who asked both Mariah and me to say yes at the appropriate times, which we did. I was asked to sign a legal document, which I did. We drove home locked into a new relationship that would terminate legally and automatically on Mariah's eighteenth birthday. "Well," I said after an unusually long silence even for us, "I guess we're stuck with each other for the next three years." I smiled to indicate that I was making a joke even though I wasn't really.

"Oh boy," Mariah said in her most monotone sarcasm ever. So I guessed the joke was on me. When our friends, family, and neighbors congratulated us on achieving our new guardianship/ward status, Mariah's response was "yeah, whatever." Although I was glad to hear something other than "lame," I couldn't ignore the way two words from this kid could suck the life out of me. The best part—Did I really say best? That might indicate some number of good parts—okay, the only positive note about being granted legal guardianship was my upgraded standing with Evergreen Academy in negotiating Mariah's matriculation. Mariah was so seldom fun to be around that I became driven to get her off to school. I was like a pit bull. Just when I was feeling particularly guilty about the selfish reasons for my doggedness in getting Mariah what *she* wanted, and feeling twice as bad about becoming her guardian and certain that it was the single biggest mistake of my life, a news story on the local channel floored me as I was making dinner that Mariah would surely not like.

There was a mug shot of Ken. He had been arraigned on charges of trafficking and possession of child pornography. The police had discovered more than a thousand images of children on his computer, some as young as four years old and some engaged in bestiality. The news described Ken as a fisherman from Isle au Haut. That hurt. The inclusion of this creep in my two most treasured identities killed me. Mariah was horrified. Her face turned scarlet and she began to cry. I spent an hour consoling her and trying to convince her that she had nothing to be ashamed of. Why did doing what I assumed was the right thing feel so awkward?

And having nothing to be ashamed of was my mantra in working with the folks at Evergreen Academy. Although some of her peers' computers had been confiscated by the police—and because kids talk, most of the school community knew a bit of the ugly story—it was a huge step for Mariah to want to return there. But as she had nothing to be ashamed of, why not? Mariah had done nothing wrong. Why shouldn't she go back with her head held high? The only glitch was that when Ken refused to let her return at the beginning of the sophomore year, Evergreen had given the twenty-five thousand dollars in scholarship money awarded to Mariah to another student who was waiting in the wings for funding. So, Evergreen reasoned, if I could pay, she could return. Not that it wouldn't have been worth it just to have my happy house back, but I didn't have that kind of money sitting in my checking account. After all, the stork had dropped this bundle of joy on my doorstep just a few weeks earlier. I hadn't had years to save and plan for the little darling's education.

Evergreen listened to my pleadings for Mariah and what was best for her. They listened as I used their own mission statement to convince them. Mariah may not have filled the bill in their "academically motivated" department, but she was the poster child for needing "help to become an independent, ethical citizen who would lead a life of purpose, action, excellence, and compassion." At the end of all discussions, the bottom line was that I would show up at Evergreen with Mariah after Thanksgiving break. I would leave her there. They would have a room for her. She would be enrolled in appropriate classes. And I would not pay. I had stepped up. And now the fine school would do the same.

I wondered whether I would make it to Thanksgiving without shooting myself in the head. Honestly, although Cowgirl had been exiled to Mariah's bedroom and bath, my entire house smelled like cat shit. I argued with Mariah on a daily basis about emptying the litter box. Why couldn't the cat shit outside? Oh, because Cowgirl is not an outdoor cat. She might get eaten by a coyote. I should be so lucky! And when Mariah *did* empty the *full* litter box, she did so nearly on the doorstep. I made the mistake of wandering into Mariah's bathroom while she was out one day (which was an anomaly in itself as she seldom left the couch unless it was begrudgingly to go to school) in search of the stench that was oozing from under her door and into my kitchen. To this day I am still wondering how the cat managed to shit on the wall. Thanksgiving could not come soon enough! Of course I would need a steam cleaner beforehand. Dingle berries are something I normally equate with the ass of a donkey. Not anymore. Cowgirl had permanent balls of shit all tangled up in her hair in her behind area. Really? Aren't cats the only things on planet Earth other than an oven that are truly self-cleaning?

Mariah did love that cat. And she looked at me as if I were a monster when I informed her that I would not keep Cowgirl when she went away to school. Sadly, I wasn't sure which of them I would be happier to be rid of, and I was immediately ashamed of the thought. Mariah didn't have shit in her hair. And she didn't stink. But her personality did. Some of her personal habits were socially frowned upon—like brushing her hair at the kitchen table—just little things we are taught when we are young, things Mariah had missed in her upbringing and that I felt responsible for teaching even if my efforts were not well received. It seemed to piss off Mariah when I scolded her or advised her about anything. She made me feel as if I were picking on her when my advice was too frequent. I didn't like nagging, but I did take my responsibility as her guardian seriously.

She really got her hackles up when I told her that she was inappropriate with men. When she wanted to get a man's attention, she always did it physically, like running her hands through a dinner guest's hair. I was relieved when Bill Clark pushed her out of his lap when she climbed in to say hi. I assumed that the way Mariah related to adults had been learned mostly from Ken. I fretted about how to help her unlearn what she didn't think was wrong in the first place, and I might have been overly cautious in trying not to offend her or hurt her feelings. One day when I witnessed her hugging the mail boat captain—a full-on embrace from chest to knees—I wanted to peel her off him. Instead, I waited until we got home so as not to embarrass her. "Hey, kiddo,"

I began, trying to lure her attention from the TV set that automatically switched on the second Mariah entered the house.

"Huh?" Mariah searched the guide for something to amuse her while she waited for dinner.

"Hey, can you turn that off for a minute so we can talk?"

"Oh. Sorry." She hit the off button and turned to face me. "What?"

This was difficult, I thought. Although I had rehearsed my opening line in the truck, I was now unsure of how to broach the subject of appropriate physical contact. It would be easier to turn the other way and not open what I assumed would be a can of worms. "I know that you really like Captain Martin, but the hug you gave him on the dock could be seen as inappropriate and might have put him in an awkward position." This was met with wide, disbelieving eyes. Maybe I should have left it at that, but as Mariah didn't respond I added, "You are a beautiful girl. You just need to be a little more careful about how you physically demonstrate feelings. I don't want someone to take advantage of your vulnerability because of what I know is innocent affection."

I watched Mariah shrink. It was as if I had beaten her and she was now cowering, looking as though she might flinch if I made any sudden moves. She kept her eyes on me as she backed into her bedroom and closed the door gently. I figured that she might be crying. God, I hoped that I hadn't read too much into her hug! What if I was paranoid and her physical actions with men were actually fine? What if I was the one who was inappropriately cold and nonphysical? My doubts were quelled the next morning when Captain Martin expressed to me his discomfort with the hug. I told him that I *thought* I had handled it, and asked that he simply push her away in the future and thanked him in advance for doing so. I expressed my opinion that Mariah's embrace had been totally innocuous and that she genuinely liked him. He agreed.

The biggest obstacle in our relationship, from my perspective, was that Mariah didn't appear to like herself. My mother always told me that if you don't like yourself, nobody else will either. I never fully understood what Mom intended for me to do with that message—still don't—but I think it was apropos in the context of Mariah. The dislike, though tolerant (because there was no other option mode), seemed to be mutual, which oddly enough eased my guilty feelings slightly. My friends and family tried to convince me that my feelings (those I dared share) were perfectly normal. I knew differently. Would I ever *like* Mariah?

I was advised by friends that I needed to have the birth control talk with Mariah. I dreaded it, but I knew it had to be done before she left for Evergreen. The memory of her reaction to my advice on appropriate hugs acted as a shock collar around my vocal cords. Each time I approached the electric fence that circled Mariah's sexuality, I got a jolt that put me back on my heels. Bif reminded me daily that Mariah might want birth control and pushed me to encourage and in fact facilitate if needed. "But don't they cover that at school? I don't remember Mom having that talk with me," I said in defense of my negative reply to my sister's question.

"You weren't sexually active at fifteen. Times have changed. Get on it!" And I knew that Bif and my friends were right. I just wanted to find the right time for a conversation that I knew would be as uncomfortable for me as it would be for Mariah.

The right time, predictably, was nearly the last minute. I don't recall why Mariah and I were aboard the *Mattie Belle* and heading to Stonington, but I knew that this trip was a good opportunity to talk because Mariah genuinely loved a boat ride. The weather was unseasonably warm, coaxing Mariah to sit on the bow with her back pressed against the windshield. Her hair seemed to love the freedom of salt air blowing through it as much as the girl did. She sang along loudly to whatever song streamed through her earphones. I chuckled at her lack of vocal ability and enjoyed her momentary, conditional happiness. When we approached the dock, she climbed around the boat's cabin and hopped down to the deck where she grabbed the stern line, ready to lasso a cleat. After we secured the boat, Mariah stepped onto the dock and offered me a hand, as she always did. It was now or never, I thought. Once we got into the Jeep she'd be absorbed in her music and texting, or napping. I grabbed her hand, let her pull me across the gap between boat and wharf, and asked, "Do we need to talk about birth control?" Mariah looked at me, puzzled, and did not answer. "Do you need to get some form of birth control?" I rephrased. "Because unless you plan to abstain, or are already using birth control, I think we need to take care of you." Now she at least looked as if she wanted to answer, but for some reason she couldn't. I understood how uncomfortable it was for her to discuss something so personal with someone with whom the relationship was *not* so personal, especially in light of the advice she had received from her last guardian. Ours was a fairly perfunctory and pragmatic relationship that did not welcome talk of caring. I reminded myself daily that I was all she had. "If you need it, we will get it." I emphasized "we."

"Okay."

Phew, I thought. No tears and no anger. "It's been a long time since I have used birth control. I'm a little out of touch. Want me to make an appointment for us to speak with someone?" I emphasized "us," and enjoyed an internal chuckle at the thought of needing birth control myself. How long had it been? . . . The chuckle quickly turned to concern for the same reason. My sexual activity was at least post-chastity-belt era. But I knew a lot had changed in the time since birth control pills were the only game in town. "I'm not prying. I just want you to be safe and protected. Okay?"

"Yes." And that was the logical place to end the conversation. We went about our business and enjoyed the boat ride home, Mariah perched this time on the stern transom, looking like any other very pretty and wholesome kid. I made an appointment with the nurse who travels to our island aboard the mission boat. She went through all of the options available, gave us pros and cons of each, and ordered a prescription. Although I was a little late in the game for the speech, I felt compelled, if I were to be any degree of parent at all, to give the one about the merits of abstinence and how she was too young for sexual relationships. I believed this to be true in Mariah's case. She at least listened politely; never even rolled her eyes or exhaled at full volume. The next time we went ashore, we picked up the prescription and I was happy to think that Mariah was protected from an unwanted pregnancy. Of course, when Mariah started bringing her packet of pills to the kitchen table when we had guests, it was time for me to reprimand her again. I told her that her birth control was a private item and should be kept in her bathroom. We were right back to the eye rolling, and "why are you picking on me?" stage. Come on, Turkey Day!

I think an innocent bystander might have observed falsely that I had been left holding the bag with regard to Mariah's health and well-being. Yes, I took sole and full responsibility for making her appointments, transporting her to them, and funding all the requisite payments. Hair, teeth, eyes, physical exam for school—I took care of everything by my own volition. But many summer residents offered financial help. My friends and family continued to volunteer assistance in any way. I took seriously my responsibility to grab the reins for the duration of Mariah's raising. I had signed a document in front of a judge. But it was more than that. I *felt* responsible for more than guardianship. Parenting was what was needed. It didn't seem right to farm that out. On the few occasions that I did accept help, it was as if I were doing the helpers a favor by allowing them to contribute. And I'll always remember that as being pretty cool. There is one guy friend in particular whom I still refer to as "Mariah's fairy godfather" because he split with me the costs of her full braces and school necessities, including books.

We went off island to do a bit of shopping for school clothes. I understood that Evergreen Academy had a dress code and that the majority of students there came from somewhat well-to-do families. I wanted Mariah to feel comfortable and not self-conscious about her clothes. God knew she had other things to worry about without having the wrong wardrobe! I couldn't help but notice while handling laundry that Mariah was in dire need of underwear. Not that she wasn't in fine shape with the amount of articles she owned, but quality and fit were not optimum. I took her to be fitted for a bra. This is quite humiliating at the age of fifteen, I learned, or was reminded. Knowing what I did about this kid's past, I suppose I should have anticipated her being prudish about purchasing underwear and undressing in front of strangers. When the sales assistant referred to Mariah as my daughter, both our jaws dropped. But we let it slide because to do differently would be too confusing and provide too much info. The salesperson handed Mariah a couple of bras in different sizes to try on and led her to a dressing room. After Mariah had been in the room for what seemed long enough, the salesperson called through the curtain, "Come on out and let's check the fit." There was no answer. "Let us take a look. It's all girls out here, honey."

The curtain opened a crack at eye level. Mariah stuck her head out and said, "And *that* would be the problem!" Slam! The curtain was drawn closed with great force. I laughed out loud while the salesperson was clearly taken aback by what I am sure was perceived as rude behavior. Well, I thought, maybe Mariah really could be my daughter. We spent the rest of the day wandering around stores, riffling through racks, and not buying much. Everything Mariah showed interest in was skimpy, too low cut, or too small for her. Everything I suggested was "lame." I tried to comment in ways that would not insult her. I never said that her choices made her look like a tramp. I pointed out that it would be cold at Evergreen. She was particularly drawn to heels when we looked at shoes. Strappy, spike-heeled shoes at Evergreen? The school is at the base of Sunday River, one of the two biggest ski resorts in Maine. I didn't expect Mariah to dress like an old lady. I mean, I didn't think she should buy tweed jackets or anything similar. She reasoned that she had attended Evergreen the winter before and knew what was permissible in the dress code. We ended up compromising on a few things, and we were both happy to be done with the shopping. The last stop we made was at Mariah's suggestion. We needed to get some shampoo for Cowgirl.

This was the best idea ever, I thought. I intended to ask Simon to take Cowgirl to Vermont, and it would be nice if his introduction to the cat at Thanksgiving made a better first impression than what I imagined was probable. Simon was a tenderhearted guy. He didn't really like cats, though. But he claimed to be my best friend, and I was in need. Need, indeed! And if he refused, Cowgirl was going to become an outdoor cat, period. I hadn't mentioned my plan to Mariah yet. No sense upsetting the apple cart. No sense ruining this otherwise joyful togetherness. I believed that Cowgirl embodied all of the bad vibes left behind by Ken. The cat skulked around the house and gave me the creeps. Ken had left behind plenty of fodder for bad memories and scary thoughts without the daily reminder from the gross cat. Simon *had* to take Cowgirl. It was a long car ride back to Stonington. When Mariah wasn't sleeping, she cranked up the radio to some rap station. She quickly changed all of the preset stations on my radio from my easy listening to her noise. Oh well, I thought, Thanksgiving is just a few day away. I was nearly rubbing my hands together.

• • •

It might have been a case of sensing light at the end of the tunnel. Or it could have been because Mariah and I were growing on each other. I'm not sure it really matters how we got there, but we seemed to have been moving to new and better ground. The days just prior to Thanksgiving weren't that bad, in a relative way. I actually looked forward to picking her up after school. And she wasn't crying herself to sleep anymore. The single rule that we followed at our evening meal together was that there was no TV. I had grown up with the rule that dinner was time for conversation. Dinner was so quiet with Mariah that I nearly rescinded the rule many times. Then, out of the blue one night at dinner, she asked, "Have I ever told you about the phone at Ken's house?" This seemed a strange conversation starter given our history of noncommunication. I resisted the urge to explain that she hadn't *ever* told me *anything*. I didn't dare respond with more than a head shaking for fear of saying the wrong thing, pissing Mariah off, and eclipsing what could be real dinner conversation. She went on to tell me about the day she was home alone and heard a clicking sound that was becoming annoying. She tracked the irritating sound to Ken's bedroom, which she was absolutely forbidden to enter, and found a recording device. She followed the wires from the device through a closet and into the phone jack in her bedroom. So Ken had been recording all of her phone calls! This girl had had no privacy at all. It was no wonder her trust threshold was sky high. I assured Mariah then and there that I had no interest in listening in on her.

"Ditto," was her response, which I chose not to take as a smart-assed statement of how she felt about anything I said (and which I was certain it was).

The next night Mariah shared with me what I would call a recurring nightmare. It sure sounded terrifying, and was certainly haunting her at the expense of solid, restful sleep. That very night I put my head on the pillow, closed my eyes, and drifted off to the horrifying image of a young girl running for her life with something evil on her heels. The girl stopped everyone she passed and begged for help. But the people she approached turned their backs to her. That was certainly an image that would not weather or fade away with time without some help, I thought. When I explained to Mariah that she had quite literally *shared* the bad dream in that I had seen it in reruns, she seemed to appreciate that I was feeling her pain. Mariah was beginning to open up a bit. She spent a night with the Clarks when I had to travel off island. Brenda reported that Mariah had asked for a notebook because she felt like writing. Mariah told Brenda that she could read what she had written, and went off to bed. Brenda read the story of a very young girl whose mother had punished her by sending her to bed with no dinner. The mother's boyfriend came to tuck the girl in. He rubbed her back and consoled the girl. "Things got out of hand, and the whole thing led to *enter-course*," she wrote. Brenda asked Mariah if she was the girl in the story. Mariah said she didn't remember. I vowed to get Mariah any counseling that was available to her for as long as she agreed to it. The calls from the social worker, Gretchen, continued. The state was willing to help if needed. But call it islandish, whether it's resistance to speed limit signs or laws governing our clam flats, we prefer to resolve our issues from within the island bubble.

. . .

'Twas the night before Thanksgiving and all through the house . . . was the sound of hysterical laughter. The time had come for the cat bath. I cringed when Mariah filled the kitchen sink with warm, soapy water, resisting the urge to scream, "Not in the kitchen!" I bit my tongue when she reached for my kitchen scissors to trim the dingle berries from around Cowgirl's buttocks. (Note to self, I thought, throw away scissors.) The cat, being a cat, did not cotton to the grooming. By the time Mariah turned on the blow-dryer, her forearms were clawed to hell and she was as wet as the cat. The blow-dryer sent Cowgirl into a real tizzy. The cat squirmed, squealed, and clawed some more while Mariah resorted to a towel. A rack of bones with long, angora-like hair, the cat looked quite hideous. Cowgirl was all eyeballs. And the eyes looked at Mariah with confusion as she forcefully towel dried her pet. "Do you suppose Simon will take her?" she asked.

"God, I hope so," was all I said as I watched the performance from a safe distance on the couch.

"Me, too," she whispered in the way that people do in front of babies when they don't want them to hear something they might understand. Mariah turned and walked away from the sink with the cat all swaddled in the towel. "She's a pretty kitty now, all clean . . . don't you want to keep her?" And she threw the cat into my lap! Cowgirl was so repulsed that all four legs scrambled and she hit the wood floor running with her tail straight up in the air, giving me a full view of what I imagined was the feline equivalent of flipping me the bird.

"Cowgirl has butt bangs!" It was the funniest thing I had ever seen. And I was laughing so hard that tears rolled.

"Linny!" Mariah screamed as if upset by my commentary on the new hairdo. It was the first time she had called me by my family nickname. It was the first time she referred to me by any name, come to think of it. We laughed together. We really laughed. This was beginning to feel like what I had imagined it might be to have a daughter. We were a small, nontraditional family unit, I thought. But we were a family unit.

The long-awaited day finally came. We had thirty people for turkey, which is the usual for my family Thanksgiving dinner. We had family and friends, including Simon, who had neither interest in nor intention of taking the clean kitty back to Vermont with him. (I knew it would be better if he came to it on his own, and I calculated how to make that happen naturally.) Fortunately, the aroma of roasting turkey overpowered the cat stench that up until now had been remarked about by everyone who had entered since the arrival of Cowgirl.

Mariah and I had our first holiday together at "our" house. I made a point of telling her every chance I got that this was now her home. She didn't need to ask before helping herself to something to eat. She didn't need to ask permission to do laundry. She didn't have to ask to use the phone. She *would* need to ask me for money when necessary, as I had no idea what her financial requirements were. When I needed money at her age, beyond what I could make doing various small jobs, I held my hand out to my parents. If I needed twenty bucks, I asked and usually received. I told Mariah that I expected her to do the same with me, and that I would provide for all her needs and some of her wants—

within reason, of course. I knew it would take time for Mariah to believe me and trust me, if she ever would. And I began to have second thoughts about sending her away to school. Our relationship was beginning to resemble something close to a caring parent/child situation. What was more important, her education and healthy social life? Or some semblance of what could be considered a maternal and nurturing family situation? I was torn. Did I really think I could do better by Mariah by keeping her with me? She had great advisers who really cared for and about her at Evergreen. The advisers and the assistant head master had become friends of mine in all of the back-and-forth discussions and negotiations. She would have access to counseling. She would have more and better opportunity all the way around at Evergreen than she would here on the island in winter. But how much of this justification was my selfishness in wanting my old life back? And now that things seemed to be improving on the home front, did I still want my old life back?

The next time Mariah and I were alone, which was Thanksgiving night after everyone had left, we were finishing up washing the mountain of dishes and talking about the fact that Simon had agreed to take Cowgirl to Vermont. It was a warm and civil talk, most of which consisted of our bolstering each other's resolve in making the right decision for Cowgirl. Simon was super nice. He would take good care of the cat. And Simon needed the company, we decided. He must certainly be lonely in Vermont. We were doing Simon a favor. I was relieved that Mariah did not mention that I would soon be alone. I would have had a hard time disguising my elation about my upcoming, much wanted loneliness. I wanted to tell Mariah that she didn't have to go to Evergreen. I should have said that I wanted her to stay home until the next year. She had been pushed away, given away, and signed away too many times in her short life. But I couldn't quite bring myself to say it. I would wait for a better time, though I knew that time was running out to give Mariah the option of staying home with me. I'm not sure what I feared more, another scathing rejection or an acceptance of an invitation that I was nervous about extending.

Sunday came and Mariah was all packed up and ready to make the journey to Norway, Maine. Simon came to collect Cowgirl that morning with a little cage he had borrowed from a friend. I had already packed the litter box, shampoo, and cat food that we had left into a box that sat by the door for a quick exit. When Mariah saw the bag of food, she said, "Geez. Shouldn't we keep the food for when Cowgirl comes back to the island?" I wanted to say that would happen only over my dead body. I didn't want to get into the conversation about Cowgirl's health and that the cat was on her last legs. It was about time for Cowgirl to do the "into the wild" thing. Isn't that what sick cats are supposed to do? But instead of telling Mariah that Cowgirl would be lucky to live long enough to breathe the Vermont air and not expire during the eight-hour ride, I offered that we could visit Cowgirl at Simon's over Christmas break from school, which was only a short time away. (Simon and I had already discussed it and were both excited about spending Christmas and New Year's at his place with our Vermont friends, all of whom, I was sure, would take to Mariah as if she were my own flesh and blood.)

And during that break we could all ski together. Wouldn't she like to learn to ski?

"Well, actually, I was talking with my mom. I think I should go home for Christmas. I haven't seen my brothers in a while. Is it okay with you?"

Ouch. You would think I'd have learned by then. Emotional disappointment frequently feels like having a Band-Aid ripped off. Simon glanced at me, shoved the cat into the cage, and left for Vermont. Well, I thought, that answers the question about whether Mariah should stay here rather than go away to school. If she is still calling Memphis home and communicating with "my mom," I should stick to the original plan. Why complicate things? And of course Christmas is all about family. I am not her mother, and I never will be. I am her guardian and want what's best for her. We should leave it there. Now I can think "good riddance" about both the cat and the kid, and not even feel guilty.

"Yeah," I said, "sure. If you want to go to Memphis for a visit, that's fine with me. Let's talk about it later. We're going to miss the boat if we don't hurry." I guessed I would be visiting Cowgirl in Vermont by myself. No possibility of hurt feelings in that relationship.

CHAPTER 9

Strings Attached

I thought that dropping Mariah at school would be just that and nothing more. She was armed with the usual accoutrements: new cell phone, computer, and a bit of spending money, all complete with what I considered necessary warnings, or as Mariah might put it, "strings attached." Evergreen Academy had a strict 10:00 p.m. lights-out policy, so the phone and computer had to be shut off at that time. I requested that she not use the phone during class, and suspected that it was forbidden by the school also. While we unloaded the car, a group of three girls came over to greet Mariah and offered to help schlep suitcases, boxes, and bags to her room. Once the hugs and giggles subsided, we all stood at the back of my Jeep and stared at one another. I was waiting for Mariah to make introductions, and I suspected her girlfriends were, too. (In hindsight, I know that they were more interested in my leaving than who I was.)

Realizing that I was the adult, and the one setting an example of good manners for Mariah, I forced the introduction. I stuck my hand out to the girl closest to me and said, "Hi. I'm . . ." And I couldn't complete the sentence. Who was I? Should I introduce myself as Mariah's legal guardian? That is so sterile, I thought. I was not her mother. I was not her friend. I stuttered. "I'm Linda," I finally blurted out. The girl shook my hand as if doing so was quite foreign to her. She never offered her name, so I didn't attempt anything formal with the other two girls, and simply nodded and smiled a cheesy take-the-picture smile. I had never felt so out of touch with a generation in my life. I had always prided myself in being comfortable with anyone of any age, any background, any ethnicity, gender preference, religion, economic situation . . . But these girls were like aliens. They were subhuman, I thought. They were poised for me to leave, so it was clear I should make my exit.

Unsure how to leave with any grace or dignity, I opened my arms for Mariah to step in with a good-bye hug. She recoiled and shrank. One or both of us would now be totally humiliated, I thought. If I drop my arms and leave, I'll be there alone. If I hug her, and she's clearly mortified, we'll be abashed in unison. Three Dog Night was surely onto something, I thought as I attempted a hug. Two *can* be the loneliest number since the number one. I have now read the thesaurus in its entirety, and there is no adjective that describes the one-way nonhug. As I let go of Mariah's tensed shoulders, she did whisper, "Awkward," which not only summed it up, but was also evidence that she had increased her vocabulary by 20 percent. Wow! And she hadn't even started classes yet.

I hadn't even left the Evergreen campus when I remembered a painful snapshot from my own teen years. My father and I were crossing a busy street in Brunswick, Maine; I was about fifteen years old, and he had had the audacity to take my arm. I broke his hold by jerking my arm out of his hand and gasping in disgust. What if someone had seen my father touch my arm? Although he never said anything, I had hurt my father's feelings. And Dad was never the oversensitive sort. I hadn't given that a thought in more than thirty years. But the memory was like salve on the new wound, and my mood brightened. Strangely, it seemed that the score had now been settled. Chalk one up for Mariah. Who knew that having a teenager could be so hurtful? Anyone who has ever survived one, I supposed. As I mindlessly drove the winding roads, enjoying some much needed windshield time, I was confused only by the fact that I was equating my relationship to Mariah with one that had always been a healthy, loving parental connection. Probably just my stunted maternal instincts run amok, I thought. The feelings might be natural, but the situation was anything but. I had always wanted children. And now that I had gone from zero to fifteen with the stroke of a pen, I had to work to shrug off second thoughts. *C'est la vie.*

The closer I got to hopping aboard my boat and heading home, the more distant Mariah's emotional snubbing of me became. I wouldn't have to deal with her again until Christmas, I thought, and even then she might go to Memphis. That, we had finally agreed, would be her call. If she wanted to spend the holidays with her biological family, I would buy her plane tickets and transport her to and from the airport. We had discussed the options at length, and had left it swaying in the breeze when Mariah couldn't decide what to do. I told her that if she had been five years old and asked my opinion of a trip west, I would have forbidden it, but at fifteen, Mariah could decide for herself what was best for her. And I had vowed never to keep her from her family or to interject too much of my poor opinion of her mother. I had never met the woman. She might be fine. I had chosen to keep our correspondence to a minimum since her dreadful reaction to why her daughter was at my house. I suspected that Mariah's mother was also a victim of abuse, knowing what I did about its being a learned behavior and a cycle that is difficult to break out of. All I knew about Mariah's biological mother was that she sometimes worked as a chambermaid but more often did not work. Mariah had lived in a hotel room, her aunt's basement, with her grandmother, in a house supplied by the church, and in a homeless shelter. She seemed to have a relatively close relationship with a grandmother and an aunt and uncle. Family is important, I knew. And no matter how much my family was welcoming and accepting of our new situation, Mariah would always have her real folks, however many really bad decisions they'd made about her or however much they'd let her down and screwed her up, et cetera. Blood ties were still important.

Home sans kid or Cowgirl . . . Being alone in my house was something I had never taken for granted, and I had now developed a real longing for it. As I slipped through the stillness in that direction, I was tempted to push the *Mattie Belle*'s throttle up to full to hasten toward the feeling of home. But it was such a dark and silent night, and the water was so calm for that time of year, that I knocked the engine out of gear and shut it down in midtransit instead. Drifting just beyond Merchant's Island—just far enough along to be perfectly positioned to see lights neither from Stonington nor Isle au Haut—I sat on the stern transom dangling my feet over the deck and breathed a sigh of relief. So much had happened in such a relatively short time. Ken was in a local jail waiting, as we all were, to learn his fate. Mariah was at a wonderful school where she would receive opportunities that she deserved. And I was on track to have my "normal" life back.

Blackness had fallen like an anchor out of a hawse pipe with the turning off of the radar and chart plotter. When my eyes adjusted to it, the darkness warmed to a degree that allowed shadows of the surrounding islands to emerge like giant whales from the inky bay. The moonless night liberated the stars in a way that can be witnessed only from a vessel floating silently at sea. Whether I was totally empty-headed or contemplating life as I knew it, it didn't matter. I could have stayed there forever. But a boat ride back to reality was imminent. I cranked the engine back up, flipped on the electronics, and headed home, carving a groove in the surface that quickly filled behind me, leaving no trace. And tomorrow morning at first light, when the bay would swell with boats buzzing around yanking traps from the bottom and splashing them back in, no one would be the wiser.

I secured the *Mattie Belle* to the mooring and zipped ashore in my skiff. My truck refused to start, requiring me to walk

home, which didn't bother me because I enjoy a walk from time
to time. I crawled between cool sheets knowing happiness. The
next day was spectacular. And if asked how so, I'm not sure I
could say. And maybe that's what was so special about it. There's
just something magical about this place—so steeped in the past,
so unchanging that it truly is the rock we refer to it as. This feeling I so often experience and can so seldom articulate may be one
that is inherent in the place we call home. But I tend to think
that it is more about what I am doing while here than the island
itself. When I am at my happiest, I feel like Thoreau when he
took to the woods to "live life deliberately." That deliberate, simple lifestyle suits me as well. I guess that is part of what I cherish
so much in being at sea. Then it hit me: This happiness that I have
while home is something that I want to share with Mariah. It is
probably something she has never had. Sure, she'll always have a
connection to Memphis, but the island will be her physical (and,
I hoped, emotional) home until she is eighteen. And after that,
she will be free to do as she pleases. Until then, I vowed that she
would have my unconditional care and guardianship. I fell asleep
embraced by the maternal part of the island that holds, consoles,
and encourages good thoughts in those lucky enough to be open
to it. And I prayed that Mariah would find openness to what it
and I had to offer her.

Sometimes life slaps you in the face. Like the nondescript
stretch of road that lulls you into heedlessness until you are suddenly at your destination with no idea or recollection of how you
got there, a period of time elapsed, leaving me with glimpses of
landmark events but no concept of the passage of days or weeks.

I literally woke up one day struggling for all my heartfelt beliefs, idealism, optimism, and life philosophies. Someone or something had pulled a weight-bearing stone from my island's foundation and things were caving. An outside force had found a chink in the island's armor and was working at it, exposing weakness. Sure, even the most virtuous among us are capable of indiscretion, but the events that littered this passage of time went beyond scandalous. I was thankful that Mariah was away at school so much of the time in the way that any guardian wants to protect her ward.

There is a surprisingly fine line separating being responsibly concerned and minding one's own business. With the Ken situation so fresh, we all questioned things when we might otherwise have just shrugged, looked the other way, or drawn the blinds. Many of us were in shock that abuse had gone on undetected and unsuspected right under our noses for so long. And then we started looking for signs of trouble everywhere. My sister Bif anguished over what she *thought* she was seeing developing in an inappropriate relationship with some underage island girls and a middle-aged man who had moved to Isle au Haut to work for the electric company. Bif *thought* she was doing the right thing by approaching the girls' mothers with her observations and concern. The mothers were by and large insulted by what my sister suggested. Her concerns were unwelcome and denied, leaving Bif questioning her own judgment and wishing she had buried her head in the sand rather than perhaps falsely accuse. Bif was still feeling the sting of the women's wrath when the electric worker allegedly committed suicide.

The authenticity of the suicide was questioned. There was a note. There was a drifting kayak. There was a wallet found precisely where the note had indicated it would be. But there was no body. And there was rumor of a sighting of the electric worker alive and well and wearing a kayak skirt on the mainland. It was all so seemingly staged, and officials didn't appear to spend much time searching. But there was an obituary. In my mind, it didn't really matter whether the man was dead or not. He was gone. He took with him some secret that would never be divulged, and one that made it impossible for him to remain here on the island. Either way, he had been a coward, to my thinking, and had taken the easy way out.

Plunging the murkiness into a shade darker was the sudden and shocking arrest of yet another island male. This one, a life-long resident, was charged with unlawful sexual contact with a minor. Some of us wondered whether island residents were now hunting witches or whether we actually had perverts under every stone. The overfriendly uncle was hauled off to jail. But he wasn't there long before an unrelated island resident bailed him out and housed him for a short time while he waited for the legal chips to fall, causing even the most demure among us to ask, "What the fuck?"

It was during this same span of time that a photograph surfaced via e-mail to me and most everyone I knew on the island with a computer. The picture was of Mariah, Ken, and Howard Blatchford. They were all aboard Howard's boat and had clearly been hauling traps because the focus of the photo was a very large lobster. The caption read "Island Daycare." I am certain that people distanced from the situation found some humor in this, but it sickened me. And it also raised the question again of whether we had an epidemic or whether our awareness of abuse had been recently heightened. Up until just recently Howard Blatchford was the only sex offender among us, or so we thought. He had made a mistake, had served his time, and now went about his business of fishing and living mostly as a partial exile. Howard had been ostracized by the community for good reason. Nobody wanted him around their children. But Isle au Haut being Isle au Haut, Howard did fish among island lobstermen, although he had been blackballed by our Lobster Association. I had always had a cordial relationship with Howard. I enjoyed an occasional conversation with him. He was a savvy fisherman. He was clever and appeared to make do with very little. I recalled how hard he worked in fighting a house fire that had threatened to total a summer home. He had nearly been in tears. But this perspective was now tainted. Seeing Mariah in this picture standing between these two men nauseated me. And it brought on a whole new onslaught of questions.

The realization that we now had three sexual offenders of children living within a scant population that had diminished to well below fifty was disheartening. When I expressed my dismay to a respected friend, his reply did nothing to make me feel better, although I know it was intended to. "We are right at the national average. It just seems like a lot because we all know one another. Most people living in other places don't *know* the child molester next door." Information like that tends to make you look at everyone differently.

There was a string of lesser disturbances that further fouled the island, or at least my perception of it. Two of our longtime residents appeared to be trying to drink themselves to death. Not that this is in any way close to sexual abuse of children, but it was another boil that came to the surface within or about this same time frame. I'm not talking about getting drunk; I am talking about getting drunk and staying that way. I am talking about being so drunk that you are found in a ditch, unable to walk or talk. Then there was a rumor that the state was coming out with drug-sniffing dogs. I have friends who smoke a lot of pot—some of whom grow their own. Now I worried that marijuana farms would be discovered and we'd be all over the local news with yet another black mark. An island high school student got pregnant. Again, not the end of the world—it happens—but I also heard that she was not certain who the father was.

Once we all adjusted to the idea of a minor having a baby, most of us remembered that babies are happy occasions, and we welcomed the new resident with open arms. We sure needed something positive in the midst of all of the badness. I even hosted a baby shower at my place that was very well attended. It seemed that every time an individual or joint effort forced something fun and positive down our throats, something evil would induce vomiting. I've got news for those who believe that bad things come in threes: This crap just kept going, on and on. Every time I spoke with friends I heard another report that made me glad Mariah was away at school. When one of my pals remarked that "we are becoming Matinicus," I couldn't muster any evidence to the contrary. Matinicus has always been the butt of jokes about incest, drunkenness, domestic violence, and drug abuse. Isle au Haut was above all of that. Or at least that's what I once believed. Disillusionment, when cast in the face of a believer as devout as I had been, hit hard.

Being an islander had always been something of a religion. And in my case, coupled with my identity as a fisherman, "islander" described what I valued most. The island had always been a sanctuary, a refuge from mainstream America. Reverent only in these two things, I longed for home while at sea as much as I longed for the sea while home. My beliefs as an islander had now been desecrated. My reverence for life at sea came to the forefront. Everywhere I looked was another sign pointing out that island life was real and hard, and not the idyllic playground I once believed it was. Some of these signs were quite literal. "For Sale" signs popped up on the lawns of summer places in what threatened to become a plaguelike scale. Were people bailing out of what they perceived as a sinking ship? Or was it just a bad economy? Some of our staunch year-rounders became seasonal residents, wintering in faraway, sunny, happy places. I couldn't pin that on economics. I thrive on hardscrabble, but minus romanticism, island life is plain old tough with no benefits.

Was this real life? I couldn't wait for an opportunity to get offshore, where it's Mother Nature you mostly have to deal with. Human nature isn't grand enough in the middle of the ocean to spoil breathtaking beauty or lessen the fear or dampen the excitement. Fishing had always been my escape from personal issues that seemed like nothing in comparison to what I had coped with lately. Until now my problems onshore had been too many men and too little money. I could cast the lines from the dock and return to home port three months down the road to no men and, I hoped, enough money to take care of what I had hastily left in payables. But I couldn't desert my problems now. A kid isn't like a utilities bill, something I could just shove in a drawer. She sure complicated things.

Friends on and off island—with and without children—told me that life with Mariah would get easier. And I actually believed them for a long time. Eventually I grew to know that my friends didn't have a clue. The second time I shut off her cell phone for not following the simple rules and for running up seven hundred dollars in overages in just one month, Mariah did seem remorseful. I just didn't understand how it was possible to send 3,200 texts in a single month while being a full-time student in a rigorous program. I got a hint when grades came out, though. To say that Mariah was not a student would be generous. She landed herself on probation at Evergreen by entertaining a young man in her dorm room—absolutely forbidden. Mariah was pretty pissed at the girl who "ratted her out," which was symptomatic of the syndrome: Nothing was Mariah's fault. Her particularly poor grades were due to "stupid teachers."

The next round of friendly advisers explained that Mariah was testing me. Testing? She'd better not make it too difficult, I thought. I might fail! And looking back, I suppose that some testing was warranted. She had no reason to trust adults. Her experience with people who had had guardianship of her, whether biological or legal, had been bleak. My opinion of her biological situation did not improve over time. Mariah did go to Memphis that Christmas, and she returned with quite a litany of horror stories, and an even worse attitude than what she had left Maine with. My first New Year's Eve with the kid was a joke. I was optimistic that December 31 would be the end of a bad year. Simon had been gracious enough to agree to celebrate with us and planned a fun night with entertaining Mariah in mind. Simon's hometown had a history of hosting quite a dazzling "First Night" gala, including a live music venue for teens. Mariah was unsure about joining total strangers at the teen event, and was unhappy about the prospect of spending her New Year's Eve with "old people." After much debate, we decided to stick together and enjoy all the activities, including dinner, music, and fireworks. Just before leaving Simon's house, and after Mariah had polished herself up for the big night, Simon read in the local news that "First Night" had been canceled. Well, this did not go over well with the princess. She bit Simon's head off and flew into a rage. It was as if Simon had somehow canceled the night himself. And Mariah hadn't been overly excited about it in the first place. But now she was in a total snit.

Rather than remind Mariah that most adults celebrate on New Year's with other adults, leaving their children home to fend for themselves with frozen fish sticks and French fries, we attempted to tease her out of her pout with the option of dinner and a movie. Mariah reluctantly acquiesced to that, citing sheer boredom as her only motivation. Simon and I were really trying to show her a good time, but were at a loss of how to do so when she just seemed so impossible to please. It was as if she had made a decision not to have fun, no matter what. She didn't like her meal, and sort of pushed items around the plate with her fork while her upper lip appeared to be frozen in a curl. Conversation was dull. While Simon paid our bill, the waitress (who must have felt our suffering) told us of a "teen skate" at the local ice arena. Mariah had never ice-skated. She said, it sounded "lame." But as we did have time to kill (and I do mean *kill*, as in put out of misery), I informed Mariah that we would at least check out the skating rink. She didn't have to skate. We would just take a look at what was going on.

Mariah reluctantly got out of the car. She followed us into the arena. We stood and watched two hundred teenage kids skate around and around to the beat of loud rap music under disco lights. Just when I was about to ask if she wanted me to rent her a pair of skates, she said, "We better go. We'll miss the movie." We left and drove in total silence for about ten minutes before Mariah said, "I'll skate if you go with me."

"Me?" I asked.

"Yes, you. I'll skate if you'll skate with me. I've never done it. But I'll try." Before I could answer in the negative, Simon was wheeling the car around in an illegal U-turn and offering to pay for the skate rentals. I couldn't possibly refuse. This was the first sign of a desire to do *anything* in so long! The next thing I knew, Mariah and I were creeping around the perimeter of the arena, arm in arm in men's hockey skates that were at least five sizes too large. She clung to me like any kid on skates for the first time, threatening to pull me down if she fell. In lap three, I found Simon watching us through the Plexiglas from the sidelines. Our eyes met. His twinkled with glee as I rolled mine in disbelief.

Mariah was a quick study on the ice, and was soon skating independent of the clutch she'd had on my left forearm. I skated beside her and enjoyed being on the ice. When Mariah sped up with confidence, I followed closely behind. When I dared take my eyes off my fledgling, I noticed kids staring at me. Some whispered and pointed. Oh yeah, I thought, I am thirty years older than everyone else here. I felt my face heat up and increased my speed to catch Mariah. I told her that I felt funny skating among teens and was going to join Simon in being a spectator while she continued. "Oh, come on! Skate a little more! Please?" When I suggested that I might be embarrassed and pointed out that too many eyes were on me, she laughed. "You have nothing to be ashamed of. You have done nothing wrong." My own words mocking me fell short of putting me at ease. Mariah's point was well taken. "Besides, these morons will never see you again." It didn't matter. I left the ice, returned my skates, and searched for Simon.

I imagined that Simon must have grown dizzy from watching us in our endless loops. He must have retired to the car, where he could listen to some real music instead of that awful noise, I thought. I sat and waited for Mariah to tire, which it seemed she never would. Every time she whizzed past my perch on the stadium seating, she looked to see if I was watching her. I gave her a smile, a thumbs-up, or a clap at each lap. Her ankles finally caught up with mine, and she gave up. We found Simon in the car, where he told us that two security guards had asked him to leave the arena. "They thought I was a pervert!" Simon was clearly shaken by this, much to Mariah's delight. She cracked up in the backseat while I confessed to Simon that the young girls were going well out of their way to avoid a huge radius of ice surrounding wherever I was. "They probably thought we were working as a team," Simon moaned in distress. This had to be very upsetting to Simon, who is known by all in the area as the very respected Dr. Holmes. Mariah's advice that I had nothing to be ashamed of reverberated in my head. But I didn't bother sharing it with Simon.

Mariah giggled all the way back to Simon's house. But her joy was short-lived. I refused to stay up and watch the ball drop on TV. So, although I had humiliated myself to please her by participating in "teen skate," I was instantly back to "lame," in Mariah's book.

Simon and I waited patiently the next morning for Mariah to get out of bed. We had promised to take her skiing. This would be another first for Mariah, and Simon and I were both hoping that she'd like it and take to it as quickly as she had the ice-skating. Simon and I are both avid skiers and wanted to share our love of the sport with Mariah. Fresh snow was falling. The conditions would be perfect! (And on the mountain Simon and I wouldn't appear as predators.) When the clock struck twelve, and Mariah had not surfaced, we agreed that a half day of skiing for the first time was more than enough.

When Mariah dragged herself to the kitchen, her eyes were still half shut. Simon greeted her pleasantly, to which he received a groan as Mariah pulled a box of cereal from a cupboard. Simon offered to make some of his special French toast for her. She shook her head and poured milk into the cereal bowl. Simon shrugged at me. I whispered that Mariah was not a morning person. He whispered back that it was one o'clock. I told Mariah that we were excited about going skiing and would leave as soon as she inhaled her breakfast. "But it's snowing," Mariah said, clearly indicating that this was a problem. "And I'm tired. I stayed up until two. That was the lamest New Year's ever."

"Happy New Year," I said to Simon. We chuckled while Mariah snarled. "We'll get our stuff packed up and leave you alone. I have to get Mariah back to school tomorrow," I said, trying not to sound too excited about the back-to-school part.

I did get her back to school. With no witnesses the parting hug was returned. And we fumbled through more holidays, long weekends, and parents' weekends at Evergreen in similar fashion—an odd threesome that observers grew used to seeing faster than we adjusted to being. Mariah seemed happiest at school. When Mariah referred to "home," I never knew where she meant—Maine or Tennessee—and that might have had some bearing on why she liked to be at school.

Over the course of two visits west, and too many phone calls from her biological mother, Mariah shared a few things that at first astounded me. The mother and brothers were in and out of a homeless shelter. An uncle was hospitalized after being beaten nearly to death. A second uncle was in jail for attempted bank robbery. The grandmother was tragically killed in a car accident at the hands of an uncle who fell asleep at the wheel. (Mariah's mom felt compelled to share details of the accident over the long-distance phone line, such as the fact that Grandma's head had gone through the windshield and her hair was embedded in the glass. Quite a scene ensued at the funeral, according to Mariah, whom I could not deny permission and funding to attend.) A female cousin exactly Mariah's age was caught sneaking out of the house and beaten so severely by her father (yet another uncle) with an electrical cord that she "couldn't wear a bathing suit for two weeks." Mariah's younger brother confessed to being sexually molested for years by an uncle who happened to be Ken's brother. Mariah was arrested along with a cousin for shoplifting during her last visit home. And this is all quite literally off the top of my head. If I thought about it, I could add to the list considerably. I would attribute all of this to white trash behavior, but I'm afraid of insulting the members of that group.

Obviously, I became hesitant to answer the phone when the caller ID indicated that Tennessee was on the other end. Mariah continued to communicate with her mother, which *did* bother me. Mariah was often upset after speaking with her mom. Although she rarely took her mother's calls in my presence, I occasionally heard their discussions through a wall or a floor. It seemed that Mariah was the mother of the two. Although I tried to convince her that she could not help her family and that she was still just a kid herself, Mariah had good intentions and a heart of gold where her immediate family was concerned. I had to admire and respect that, and I thought Mariah's gut instincts were spot on. But the question about nurture or nature loomed. I had endless discussions with myself about *terroir,* and whether people, like grapes and coffee beans, are products of the soil and environment in which they are raised. Are characteristics bestowed during early development overcome when there is a change in climate? When, if ever, is it too late? I tried not to lecture Mariah. I tried to set a good example and knew that my associations—both friends and family—set great examples. But in light of Isle au Haut's recent activities, I wondered whether this climate change was conducive to healthy change and growth, which I had always believed it to be.

The answer to that would come in time. Sure, the island had slipped in a big way. But there was still such an abundance of goodness here that I had to believe the black cloud would give way to light. And there was no place else I wanted to live other than at sea. And continuing my part-time gig at sea was something else I needed to figure out. With my island identity in the balance, I would feel even more of a draw to blue water. Normally I could sling my seabag onto the deck of a boat and head offshore at a moment's notice. There had been times when I had left for sea without saying good-bye to anyone, and only called my family after the lines had been cast. That nonschedule might be a little tricky with my new acquisition.

I had been struggling for some time with the seemingly contradictory impulses of pulls from the sea and shore, and trying to find the right balance. Mariah's presence in my life made finding it that much more difficult. I was never so tempted to hop aboard a boat and leave my troubles behind as I always had as I was now. No, I thought, it would be irresponsible to go fishing and leave Mariah to someone else's watch. Wouldn't it? But chasing swordfish was my passion. Had pursuing my own happiness been eclipsed when I'd taken charge of Mariah? Was this what mothers everywhere mean when they talk about sacrificing for their children? Was I willing, or even able, to give up my life for the betterment of someone else's? And who's to say that my being around was best for Mariah? Maybe she'd be better off with me as an absentee guardian. Maybe someone with prior experience could step in for three months every fall while I went to work offshore. I did need to continue to make a living in order to provide Mariah with what she required. Sure, in the state of Maine guardians are not obligated legally to provide financial support for their wards from their own resources. Although I chose not to go that route, there are ways to get subsidies and health care. I remembered that from our fifteen minutes in court. Sure, the state prefers permanent guardianship, "assuring long-term care that is as nurturing and stable as possible," to foster care. And all that was required of me as that permanent guardian was to show an "ability to provide nurture, protection, and stability," which seemed both vague and minimal to me. But I did *feel* as though I was Mariah's support, emotionally as well as financially. And I wanted to do my best for her. I understood that the state of Maine had to allow guardians and foster care parents some leniency regarding financial obligations, without which there would be even more unwanted orphans. I understood that I was obligated to keep Mariah fed, housed, and clothed (with no specific standards). But I wanted to provide Mariah with much more. I wanted her to have opportunity, and that sometimes comes with a price tag. Besides, who else would pay the cell phone bill? Sure, a cell phone is not a *need*, unless you are willing to let your child be a total misfit among peers. I wanted normalcy for Mariah, and was willing to foot the bill for some of what that required.

Funny, I used to laugh when I heard people expressing how having children changed their lives and complicated things. Really? I was so accustomed to dealing with forces so much grander! How much could feeding and changing diapers actually change *you*? And to what degree could one little person complicate life? I was just beginning to understand. Hell, I didn't even know how to introduce myself anymore. I guess things *have* changed. And to think that motherhood was something I had *wanted*. It was something I thought I had missed out on. Another example of being careful what you wish for, I thought. And there it was. I had to continually check myself. I was not Mariah's mother. I would never be her mother. This was a temporary situation. My guardianship of Mariah would legally terminate on her eighteenth birthday. If things didn't improve drastically, it could be a very long three years.

All the while during this temporary interruption to life as I knew and wanted it came snippets of news about the federal government's case against Ken. These, too, littered that vague span of time from end to end. It was now clear that Ken had gone to great lengths to tamper with Mariah's head. The hard-drive evidence showed that Cody (the young e-mail friend who had coerced Mariah to pose for and send nude photos), the unnamed women in Texas who forwarded a picture of Ken's erect penis to Mariah, and Marie (the French cybersex partner of Ken's who was relentless in abusing Mariah in e-mail correspondence— complete with broken English) were all fabrications of Ken's. All of this inappropriateness, crudeness, and filth had been generated exclusively by Ken on his computer. All of this further illuminated the psychological perversion of Ken and how he had dedicated his life to ruining Mariah's.

With a court-appointed attorney, Ken tested every legal avenue available to him for release from jail while awaiting trial. We were notified each time he had a hearing. My sister Bif attended many of the hearings and reported back to me that each attempt had failed. He even asked a judge to release him to a third party! I was extremely nervous about who might vouch for and be responsible for this creep. I prayed it wasn't anyone Mariah and I knew. I prayed that the judge would not allow his release. A convicted felon in a wheelchair was the best that Ken could suggest as a third-party custodian. His final hearing for bail was denied. When I relayed that good news to Mariah, she suggested that perhaps now her nightmares about his sudden appearance at Evergreen might subside.

The volcano of events that had erupted beginning with Ken had certainly been belching a putrid breath. Sometimes the stench had come in a gale of wind from Memphis, and sometimes it was more indigenous. Mariah and I did begin to bond in our shared resolve to simply endure the stinking times. During that obscure passage of time (studded with explicitness best marked by promises and threats related to cell phone use) I became Mariah's conduit to the legal process and proceedings. Like a buffer, I absorbed happenings and relayed what I thought she should or needed to know. I held some things back for her emotional protection. And I was forthright in telling Mariah that I would not share things I felt needn't be. She was good with that. I told Mariah that I really *wanted* to take care of her. I think I talked a pretty good game. I kept second thoughts, which were becoming less frequent, to myself. Outwardly I was being a parental figure, perhaps the only one she had ever had. I assured Mariah that *my* job as guardian was to take care of everything, and that *her* only job was to behave and do her best at school. Tenure was not in the cards for either of us.

CHAPTER 10

A Package Deal

With a characteristic total lack of pageantry, Cowgirl simply died. A far cry from the cats of my childhood that got dramatically caught in the car's fan belt or the spokes of a speeding bicycle (which didn't do a lot for the rider's knees and elbows), Cowgirl had something in common with March: out like a lamb. There was none of the high-volume screeching that an injured-in-combat and soon-to-be-dead cat emits. There was no dramatic hanging on by the claws from the edge of death or heroic attempts to resuscitate. No, Cowgirl's exit was more of a silent riding off into the sunset, unnoticed. As Simon hadn't actually witnessed the cat's exit from the stage of life, the thought crossed our minds that she might have been stolen. Then I recalled her appearance and nearly fell out of my chair laughing. More than likely, Cowgirl had simply slinked off into the woods surrounding Simon's house in Vermont, never to return.

It wasn't that Simon hadn't put forth major effort in keeping Mariah's cat alive. In fact, at last tally Simon reported spending in excess of $1,200 in health care for the cat. Maybe it had something to do with the Hippocratic oath taken by Dr. Holmes so many years ago, but I just couldn't get my head around his willingness to pay the enormous vet bills. I understand that it was indeed humane of Simon to deworm and de-flea Cowgirl. And it was kind of him to experiment with different types of kitty litter (all purporting to eliminate odors), and it was certainly within reason to serve a variety of high-end cat foods until finding one that suited Cowgirl's discerning palate. But it's quite another thing to have the cat receive every shot she'd never had, knowing that she was clearly on shaky ground in a "not long for this world" type of way. And I would have drawn the line well before collecting and delivering a stool sample. The diagnosis resulting from a myriad of tests was hyperthyroidism, which required Dr. Holmes to administer to Cowgirl some oral medicine. The pills were not well received, and when Simon's hands were scratched and bitten to pieces, he went back to the veterinarian for an alternative treatment (for the cat). The vet recommended some medicated ointment. (This part is hard for me to believe, but Simon had no reason to exaggerate.) He had to administer the ointment to one of Cowgirl's ears daily, alternating ears. Simon kept track of left or right on his desk calendar. It was suggested that Simon was more attentive to Cowgirl than I was to Mariah. To that I took offense.

The problem to my mind was not that the cat had passed, but how and when and who would tell Mariah. This was something that Simon and I agreed might send Mariah into hysteria as we shared an opinion that she was quite fragile emotionally. We fretted about sharing this sad news for weeks, avoiding any conversation that might lead to her asking, "How is Cowgirl?" Avoiding conversation altogether was most manageable from my perspective, as I had not yet turned Mariah's cell phone back on after her most recent abuse of use and coinciding gigantic overage bill. So now it appeared that Simon had gotten the better part of *that* deal. Simon had paid his last vet bill. His obligations of responsibility were done. Mine were ongoing. Not that I would equate child rearing with pet responsibility. But there are similarities that come to mind when I think about it in the shallows of my pool of thoughts. I was pretty happy to have a healthy kid! Well, fairly healthy anyway (healthy by everyone's standards but her own).

I wouldn't say that Mariah was a hypochondriac, but she seemed to spend an inordinate amount of time with the nurses at Evergreen Academy. I received calls from the school clinic, biweekly at a minimum, for anything from a cough to chest pain. Mariah saw a doctor when the nurses deemed it appropriate, and also had a weekly appointment with a counselor off campus. In addition to the school's health care professionals, I spoke on a regular basis with Mariah's advisers, who were good about, well, advising. So my communication with Mariah was through a conduit, and rarely between the two of us.

I did try to call Mariah on her room phone, mostly to no avail.

I figured that she refused to answer, in case it might be me, in an attempt to frustrate me to the point of turning her cell phone back on. She eventually won this contest because I was starting to feel bad about talking about her rather than with her. I reconnected her cell service and dialed the number prepared to tell her about the passing of her beloved Cowgirl. Mariah picked up the phone on the first ring. Amazing, I thought, because the phone had been shut off for several weeks. "Oh, Hiiiiii," she said in what I might have mistaken as sarcasm, but it could have been genuine delight *not* in hearing my voice but rather in the knowledge that she could now text her brains out until the next billing cycle. I asked how she was, to which she responded in great length and detail about her many physical ailments, including the pain in her chest that her counselor attributed to anxiety because the doctor had ruled out any biological cause. "But," she continued, "I am feeling lots better now that my phone is back on." Yeah, right, I thought, nothing short of a miracle. Carpal tunnel syndrome is preferable to anxiety-driven chest pain. She told me that the doctor had recommended some prescription medicine for her anxiety, and for that she needed my permission.

This is where I stalled. I wasn't sure about prescription medicines for anxiety and/or mood swings at the age of fifteen. Aren't girls that age naturally anxious and moody? Every time I had mentioned what I considered extreme symptoms displayed by Mariah to the girlfriends in my new island advisory committee, they had unanimously responded that all was quite normal. Even when I chose to argue that Mariah exhibited behaviors I considered deep in the abnormal realm, they laughed and confided that it could and probably would get worse, citing examples of the atrocities they'd experienced at the hands of *their* daughters. Of course we all shared concern about the extent of damage years of abuse by Ken might have caused. But for now I had to stick with the plan of getting on with things, moving forward in a positive manner with shades of Frank Sinatra: "Each time I find myself flat on my face, I pick myself up and get back in the race. That's life . . ."

Was medicine a cop-out? Didn't Mariah need to ride the bronco into adulthood unadulterated? But I also knew that pain from anxiety is real, and perhaps Mariah was suffering unduly and medicine was appropriate. She couldn't put her finger on what was bothering her or what she might be stressing about. There was no doubt in my mind that her anguish was a direct result of what she had endured at the hands of Ken, and that it would be something she would deal with for a very long time with the help of the professional counseling I was happy to provide for as long as she wanted. I juggled options for a minute and finally went with my gut. I suggested that Mariah wait a bit before starting on medication. I shared my opinion that drugs were the easy way out and that perhaps coping skills could not be developed if symptoms were masked rather than dealt with and overcome. I reminded her that she claimed to like and benefit from her sessions with her counselor and encouraged her to continue these and even increase the frequency of visits if she wanted. Mariah sounded a little disappointed that I would not give permission for the prescription at this time and mentioned some number of friends who had prescription mood levelers, which did nothing to sway me. I agreed that we would revisit the topic when she came home for her next break and that I would certainly set up an appointment with a doctor for a second opinion at that time if she still felt a need.

When we hung up, I realized that it would have been much easier to permit drugs to be prescribed. I wouldn't need to deal with it again. I found solace in knowing that if Mariah were my own flesh and blood, I would have responded in the same way. So here I was again acting like the mom that I wasn't. I was relieved to have had a legitimate excuse not to mention Cowgirl. No sense fueling the anxiety, I reasoned. Inwardly I believed that the death of this cat was ultimately a good thing in that it was a reminder of a nasty past. But I am not an animal lover. Mariah is. In fact, the only time I had seen real joy in Mariah was when she was petting a dog or ogling newborn kittens. I wouldn't lie to Mariah. If she asked, I'd tell her that Cowgirl was gone. But otherwise I would wait for a better time. The question did arise in my mind about whether I was protecting Mariah or myself from her reaction. I decided to give myself the benefit of the doubt this time.

The next phone call wasn't the right opportunity either. This conversation was another plea for medication. The chest pain had subsided, but now Mariah had stomach issues. She had indigestion or something like it. "Stuff" was coming up in her throat and gagging her. She even threw up! She needed prescription medicine, she said. I suggested that she should try Tums first. I was afraid that Mariah would think I wasn't taking her ailments seriously, so I made an appointment for her to see a GI specialist, a friend of Simon's who agreed to squeeze her in for a work-up during a long weekend at home she had coming soon. Mariah seemed to be growing increasingly annoyed with my refusals to allow her to start popping pills. I was growing increasingly nervous about the amount of time that was passing since the death of her cat and my not telling her. Each time I saw her name on my caller ID, I quickly vowed to spill the beans. But I always hung up without doing so. The longer my silence on the topic persisted, the more difficult it became to bridge the gap between living cat and dead cat. The next call was a complaint of sleeplessness, which could be remedied by sleeping pills if I could be so kind as to agree. No way.

During this time of phone off and phone on and calls from the school nurses, the island was relatively quiet, as it usually is in late March. I had learned long ago that happenings on Isle au Haut were somewhat episodic in that they came in waves (not in threes!). We seemed to be in a trough right now. Other than the usual gripes and grudges, there were no new surges of good or bad—all was copacetic. Oh sure, there were minor disturbances that rose from the ashes of longtime disputes. And those served to keep life interesting. One ember that was fanned to a small flame involved me, indirectly.

I was off island to do a speaking event when my sister Bif called to inform me that she had just spoken with a friend on the island who had told her of the good deed he had done on my behalf. It had snowed about a foot and a half of wet, heavy flakes and the weather was predicted to get very cold. The friend had taken it upon himself to shovel out my truck, which awaited my return in the town parking lot. If he hadn't cleared the snow from on and around my vehicle, he thought it might just stay put until spring in the iceberg that would form with the dropping temperature. This was nice. And if he hadn't added that he had, in the process of shoveling my truck out, absolutely buried the vehicle of someone else, I would have thanked him. "You can't even see the top of the antenna! That car won't see daylight until the Fourth of July!" I supposed this little act of kindness was retaliation for something. On Isle au Haut, grudges are held dear, often longer than the disgruntled can remember what the cause was. I was put out, only for fear of having the owner of the ice-encrusted vehicle point a finger of blame my way.

That night, planning to return home the next morning to my cleanly shoveled truck, I received a call from the wife of the owner of the entombed car. I hesitated to pick up, but realized that it might be worse if I did not. Might as well face the mis-aimed wrath now and deny, deny, deny. I wouldn't need to throw my friend under the bus because my alibi was solid. I was not on the island at the time of the storm or subsequent mischievous shoveling. The wife apologized for bothering me but thought I might like to know that her husband had borrowed my truck to go home in because he couldn't begin to break the ice from his own. I wasn't going to need my truck anytime soon, was I?

The next time I left my truck at the dock, I took the keys with me—something I had never before done. This trip was to pick up Mariah at school and head for Vermont to visit Simon and the GI doctor whom we no longer needed to see. I had four hours in the car with Mariah in which to tell her about Cowgirl. But

Mariah cranked up the music, put her seat back, and fell fast asleep. With her most recent complaint in mind, I didn't have the heart to wake her. I glanced at her from time to time and felt a strange emotion I hadn't felt before. I was taking some degree of comfort in Mariah's peacefulness. I wondered if this was what parents felt when standing over a crib smiling and sighing at their child and speculating what dreams might be dreamed and how the child would pursue them. Some hopeful wonderment about Mariah's future tiptoed around my head, careful not to disturb. I resisted the urge to push Mariah's bangs away from her eyes.

Mariah stretched and yawned about the time we rolled into Simon's driveway. It was now inevitable, I thought. Simon came out to greet us. After a sleepy "Hi" from Mariah, the next thing I heard was "How's Cowgirl?" Simon's jaw dropped. His eyes opened wide and he glared at me with a questioning look. I guess I had neglected to tell Simon that I hadn't found the right time to deliver the sad news.

I took a deep breath and braced myself. "I'm sorry I didn't tell you sooner, but Cowgirl died."

I heard myself swallow in the silence that followed. Mariah frowned and her eyes crinkled at the corners. Her lower lip began to quiver. Emotion was building palpably. Simon wandered into the garage and pretended to putter with something. When Mariah shifted her focus from the ground at her feet, our eyes met. I was more than prepared to console Mariah as I had rehearsed this so many times. I took a deep breath. She opened her mouth to speak and said, "Can we get a dog?"

I suppose there was some sense of relief. But what I felt most was pissed off. My maternal instincts had been cheated once again! Mariah needed none of the comforting, cheering, or soothing that had lain dormant in me for so long and now beat at the door begging to be unleashed. She didn't want sympathy or knowledge of cause of death. She didn't want to hear that Cowgirl had gone to the big litter box in the sky. She didn't want to place a wreath or a cross as a memorial. She didn't want to reminisce about the good times she had shared with Cowgirl, or publically contemplate what a good cat she had been. Mariah wanted a dog. "No" was all I could muster.

"Why not?" I turned on my heel and headed into the house while fully explaining why not. For starters, Mariah could not keep a dog at school. My schedule did not allow for a dog—too much time away from home, traveling, fishing, et cetera. And even if I were a stay-at-home mom, I did not *want* a dog. "Oh, that is so mean! Come on, please? Look, I have a picture of a pug on my phone. Isn't he the cutest?" Mariah followed close behind me, pleading all the way like the kid in the grocery store who had just been told no by his mother about the box of Ring Dings. "I promise I'll . . . ," and she went through the usual litany of covenants associated with pet care.

"That's what I said to *my* mother when I wanted the ant farm. She has never forgiven me for releasing them to live in my sock drawer. Of course she'd have never caught on if I hadn't fried the vacuum cleaner trying to recapture them. Damned socks!" Mariah didn't find nearly as much humor in this as I did. And the pleading continued until it was a full whine. When I couldn't take any more, I pushed Mariah toward Simon. He was a softer touch than I was in these matters. After all, he had been suckered into the cat ploy. The wanting of a dog became Mariah's mantra. It is truly the only thing other than prescription medicine that she was persistent in asking for and didn't receive. And so Cowgirl's uneventful, undramatic passage was appropriately celebrated with no sharing of sorrow, no condolences, no lamentation, and no grieving.

Not so, the death of Uncle George. The dearth of pathos surrounding Cowgirl's expiration stood in abrupt juxtaposition to the emotional tsunami that encompassed George's demise. Uncle George, the last of my dad's siblings, received the full fanfare that the Greenlaw family has become known for. Not that we are an overly religious group, but we do have our signature ceremonies that resemble a production requiring great orchestration. Most of the hoopla surrounding a (I hesitate to call it a funeral because it would not qualify in most people's minds) family burial is due to the location of the graveyard and logistics of the physical act of burying.

Uncle George had expressed two wishes before he died: One was to be buried alongside his mother (my grandmother Mattie) and his sister (my aunt Sally) on Isle au Haut, and the other was to have his father there, too. His father, my grandfather Aubrey Greenlaw, had been dead for twenty years and was buried with his second wife in Woolwich, Maine, a small town on the mainland. In order to grant wish number two, Gramp had to be disinterred and moved to the island, where he could be replanted. Readers of *The Lobster Chronicles* may recall that my grandmother required two burials also, placing my paternal elders in a class remotely akin to perennials. Of course we all believed that the rising of Gram (on her own accord) from the grave after she was planted was in response to my grandfather's remarrying before her body was cold. So the disinterment of her gadabout husband seemed justified. Rest in peace evidently means nothing to my family.

When I say we bury our dead, I mean that we all take active roles in what is more of an escapade than a solemn event. Because digging graves on the island is such a frig—the island is mostly ledge—it seemed wise and frugal to excavate one big hole to accommodate both caskets rather than go through the process twice. We all marveled at George's insistence on not being cremated. Aunt Sally, our most recent death, wisely chose cremation and was "put in with a posthole digger." That was relayed by Sally's widower, Uncle Charlie, while we worked as a family with chain saws to clear a path for the backhoe for Uncle George's procession. Fellow islander and friend Al Gordon was the man with the equipment to clear trees from and excavate the site, and he did so with competence and respect for both the dead and living Greenlaws. It made sense to organize the hearses to the dock, and boat to the island, in a way that would require one trip. So two hearses rolled down the dock in Stonington, and two caskets were lowered hydraulically aboard the *Mattie Belle.* Two pickup trucks received the caskets and delivered the two corpses to the grave site. It wasn't long before my sister Bif was referring to the service as a "twofer."

At the edge of the hole my dad said words remembering his brother and father fondly, and he was pretty choked up. That's a hard thing to witness when you've never seen your father shed a tear. But the cracking of his voice was soon forgotten when nine-year-old Addison took the floor. When asked if anyone else wanted to speak, we all looked around, fearful that one of us might *have to*. Addison sauntered to the front of our small crowd, hands jammed in hip pockets, turned to face us, and said, "I didn't actually know him very well, but he was a good grandfather." That was it. He returned to his position between his father and grandfather. It was simple and direct. We had no idea which of the two men Addison eulogized. And if either George or Aubrey had been Addison's grandfather it wouldn't have been funny at all. Come to think of it, Addison was likely confused by the whole twofer thing. The event didn't become a fiasco until we couldn't remember which casket was which or which end was head and which was foot. I recall discussion that wasn't heated enough to denote argument as we worked with shovels to throw dirt back into the holes after the coffins were not so smoothly lowered. To this day we aren't sure who is where or which way, which brings back memories of Gram's burials (yes, both of them).

Mariah's take on her first experience with the death of a member of her new family was that it was "different." And with that I could not disagree. Simon was kind enough to transport Mariah to and from school for the festivities because he had to go right by Evergreen in his travels, saving me the time and effort. Mariah hadn't spent much time as an integral part of the Greenlaw clan. My parents were polite but hadn't yet bonded with Mariah in any significant way. Looking back, I am sure that my mother was being protective of me because she was certain that my assuming guardianship was a huge mistake with which I would have to live for another three years. My dad loves to tease lightheartedly. His attempts with Mariah were met with tears, which made my father feel very bad because he would never intentionally hurt or upset anyone. And my time with Mariah took time away from Mom and Dad. Although it wasn't spoken about, Mariah's presence seemed like a wedge that threatened to divide a close and solid family unit. This was probably just in my mind, but I think it bears mentioning. As much as my parents wanted to protect me, I wanted to protect Mariah.

If anything, maybe I was feeling guilty about spending less time with aging parents, and I had Mariah to help justify it. The bottom line was that while I may not have been the ideal mother figure, I did have an uncanny ability to surround Mariah with greatness from other sources. My family was more than welcoming to anyone who showed interest in being part of us. The confusing thing was that it was not evident that Mariah wanted a part. Other than our somewhat strange dealing with our dead, I see us as a shining example of a strong, loving, and perpetually optimistic and supportive unit. The island population as a whole was genuinely interested and active in my relationship with Mariah, and seemed to have a vested interest in what we all hoped would be our ultimate success. My neighbors and fellow community members were consistent in checking in with me and Mariah. When Mariah was home with me, we received dinner invitations that we enthusiastically accepted and always had great follow-up conversations afterward. Mariah was beginning to be sort of fun to be around. I think she was becoming more comfortable in our unorthodox unit. Although we had a vast distance to cover, I felt that we were gaining baby steps in the right direction.

Simon and Mariah seemed to be bonding quite nicely. And I couldn't have been happier about Simon's help with her, even though it confused the issue of my wanting to terminate our existing relationship and revamp. Simon had become the closest friend I could ever imagine having, and I wanted very much to retain that while moving forward with someone else on a romantic level. I had no idea who that someone else might be, but I wanted to be open to an opportunity if I should happen upon one. I suspected that Simon felt the same way but had no way of really knowing because we never talked about it. I couldn't imagine anyone serving as a better father figure for Mariah. Simon is kind, generous, smart, hardworking—all of the things you want your children exposed to. And Simon has a stick-to-itiveness that I respected, especially in his not accommodating Mariah's ongoing dog request, but at the same time, I was frustrated by it in other facets of life. I hoped that I wouldn't take Mariah's feelings into consideration to a degree that shaded my decisions on how to proceed with Simon. If we "divorced," how would that affect the stability that I knew was paramount to Mariah's well-being? Many couples stay together for the sake of children, but Simon and I weren't married. And Mariah wasn't really ours, was she? I could, I reasoned, always date a guy with a dog.

When my cluttered web of emotional confusion embodied jointly in Simon and Mariah sped away from the town dock headed for Vermont, I breathed a sigh of relief that signified deliverance from the burden of figuring things out. In the world of clichés, this was not "out of sight, out of mind," but rather a "sweeping under the rug." Items under the rug are still there. Know what I mean? But I felt that I could now postpone dealing with the mess I had created and stored in my psyche regarding my two most prominent relationships and concentrate on the easier and more fun ones linked to my sisters. There would always be time later to pull back the rug and get the broom out.

I think that sisterly love is one of those things that are impossible to articulate. So I won't try. If you don't have a sister, you wouldn't get it anyway. And if you do have a sister, you don't need an explanation. I am lucky to have two sisters, Bif and Rhonny, and was most fortunate at the time of the double burial to have both of them on the island with me. Rhonny, two years my senior, had moved (on a whim) to Florida and was now home for an extended, undefined visit that we had all come to expect of her. I recall stretching out in the middle of my large, sectional sofa, flanked by sisters, and just letting all guards down. Sisters can and do talk about everything. We laughed about the twofer, cried about the twofer, and sat silently contemplating the twofer. The silence was finally broken when Bif asked about Mariah.

I spoke openly and honestly about my perception of our relationship, my hopes for her future, and my fear that I was not doing a very good job as guardian. "It just doesn't feel right. You know what I mean? I guess I was hoping to become more of a mother figure than just the person who provides basic needs until she's a legal adult. I want the best for Mariah. She deserves opportunity, and I hope I'm providing that."

Both sisters chimed in with verbal pats on my back for taking on such a project and congratulated me on hanging in there when things were rough. "Yeah, I remember thinking the same thing about Mattie when she was fifteen," Rhonda confided about my niece, who was now out of college and holding down a job in graphic design. "Mariah will come around. She is a very lucky girl to have you."

"She is lucky. I'll agree with you there. She is most fortunate to have this entire community and Greenlaw family and network of friends to support and bolster both of us. But she's just so stubborn! Sometimes I feel like choking her, at others I feel like hugging her, and once in a while I just feel like throwing my arms in the air and walking away," I confessed. "But of course I'll never do that. That would be admitting that I made a mistake. Not happening."

"Linny," Bif started, "you know that we will help in any way we can. Right, Rhon?" Rhonda nodded enthusiastically. "I assume you'll need or want to go fishing next fall, and I'll be available to get Mariah back to school for you and act as guardian until you get back ashore."

"Yup. Want *and* need. I'll need the income to continue to pay the bills around here, and I'll want to get back to what I love and to live within my comfort zone for a while. This whole thing just feels so awkward. I always assumed that being a mother would come naturally. I was wrong."

"When women give birth, the relationship is clearly defined as between mother and child. This is different. You can *mother* Mariah. But you can't *be* her mother. What do you *want* your relationship to be?" Bif asked. The question had never been posed. And I realized at that instant that I needed to define what I wanted and stop pussyfooting around the issue of why, in my mind, our relationship wasn't working. How could it work if I didn't even know what it was?

I wasn't willing to sacrifice what I loved most in the world for this kid, and had been torn about it. Now, in light of Bif's suggestion to define the relationship in my own way, even if unorthodox, I could give myself permission to do my thing offshore knowing that it would be best for both Mariah and me. I wanted Mariah to be happy. I assumed that she would not be opposed to my being happy. I admitted to being happiest when I was home alone while Mariah was at school. My sisters said that it was okay for me to feel that way. Because they are my sisters, I believed them. Rhonny offered to host Mariah in Ft. Lauderdale for all or part of any winter breaks from school, or to stay at my place with her in the summer if I needed to be away on a book tour. We fell silent again.

Completely relaxed, I lounged on the sofa and thought, wow. Not only have I provided Mariah with her basic needs, a supportive community, an exclusive education, a wonderful father figure, and a devoted and close network of friends and family, but I've also provided two of the coolest aunts ever. This package deal was more than even the best mother could offer a child, I thought. Our collective silent reverie was shattered when Bif sprang from prone position to fully upright and then to her feet, shrieking, "Get it off me! Oh my God, get it off!"

Rhonny and I both bolted upright and chased the now running Bif around the house trying to see what was on her that she needed to get off. As Bif is very squeamish, I wasn't really all that alarmed that she was freaking out. We finally caught her in the kitchen and I asked, "What?"

Her eyes showed real terror and she held her left elbow in her right hand as she screamed, "A tick! A fucking tick! Get the fucker off me!" (Bif doesn't normally use foul language, which makes it hard to believe she is part of my family.) I squinted at the spot on Bif's upper arm that she was now pointing at.

"I think it's a pimple," I said.

"It's moving! It's not a fucking pimple! Oh my God, it has legs! Get it oooooofffff!!" Rhonny and I agreed that neither of us could actually see well enough without our reading glasses to determine what tiny spec stuck to Bif's flesh was sending her through the roof. I hustled to find a pair of glasses, donned them, and saw clearly that the spec did indeed have legs that were moving. Rhonny inspected with my glasses and confirmed that it was a tick and that the tick was in the process of burrowing itself into Bif's arm. Bif was now beyond panic and babbled endlessly about Lyme disease and the fact that she could not miss a minute of work for any reason. Rhonny had loads of experience removing ticks from the many dogs she had owned through the years, and suggested burning the tick with a cigarette to get it to back out of Bif's arm or covering it with Vasoline to suffocate it into backing out. Bif was now getting pale and breathing way too hard. "Linny, just please get it off me. NOW!!!!" All we had ever heard about Lyme disease was that it is imperative to get treatment quickly. We knew that if untreated, the disease could be quite debilitating. We assumed that Bif had picked up the tick at the grave site the day before. I ran upstairs and grabbed a pair of tweezers. I squeezed the tick and pulled. It broke in half. I showed Bif the half tick that was now stuck to one end of the tweezers. "Are you fucking kidding? Come on! Let's go to Kate and Steve's. They'll know what to do."

The three of us marched over to the neighbors' place, where they were busy getting the morning coffee and pastries together for early visitors to the café. We barged through their front door and explained Bif's dilemma. Bif was somewhat quieter now, but had to divert her eyes from the end of the tweezers when I showed Kate and Steve what I had managed to extract. Kate and Steve began by telling me what I had done wrong. Apparently the proper technique was to twist while pulling, sort of like uncorking the embedded tick from flesh. Now that there was nothing of the tick exposed to grab for another try, an incision would be necessary. While we discussed how Bif should see a doctor for this—during which she adamantly refused, citing her need not to miss any work as she had a business to run—Bill and Brenda arrived. Bill likes to toss gasoline on a fire. He never misses an opportunity to tease. His thoughts on the situation added a sense of urgency even though I knew he was kidding. When he spoke of the possibility of tick eggs being laid in the arm, I fought back a laugh. Bif looked as if she might puke.

Before Bill was done talking about Lyme disease, its symptoms, and what Bif's eventual prognosis would be, Bif was right back to screaming profanities. She now insisted that we get a scalpel and perform surgery on her arm immediately. Nancy Calvert, who is a trained nurse, was the logical choice for a surgeon because Simon had left with Mariah early that morning. Steve placed the call and Nancy and Bill Calvert arrived in short order, scalpel and magnifying glass ready. Nancy, Bill, and their dog had all suffered from Lyme disease, so their input was valuable. I'm not sure who suggested vodka shots, but Bif was more than happy to take a couple of belts before Nancy dug in. While she dug at the spot with the tip of the scalpel (after sterilizing it with a lit match), Rhonny and I each slugged down a shot of vodka. It was a sister thing (like shaving your head because someone you love lost hair in chemotherapy). Nancy was trying to be careful, not wanting to hurt Bif. When Bif screamed, "Just fucking do it!" Nancy plucked the remainder of the tick from her arm with a quick, deep thrust and a jerk. The three sisters toasted Nancy with yet another round of vodka that no longer burned going down.

We left Kate and Steve's with two halves of a tick in a baby food jar and strict instructions for Bif to see a doctor when she got back home the next day and that she should send the tick to the state for toxicology. We all knew that neither would happen. But Bif clutched the jar like a prize she had won, placing it on my coffee table for all to see when we relayed the story, which we did several times that day. I had seen a member of my fishing crew with a mako shark latched onto his calf muscle react less than Bif did to the tiny tick. Now that her hysteria had subsided, we could chuckle. The three of us lollygagged on the sofa until bedtime that night, reliving old times and forecasting the future the way middle-aged sisters do. And it seemed we hadn't a care. We were comfortable in our laziness, and didn't mention that we would part ways the next morning not knowing when we'd share another laugh. The tick episode had taken center stage, but the issue of my relationship with Mariah was still waiting in the wings. But I had made a very conscious decision. I did not want to be merely Mariah's guardian. I wanted and would *mother* her, though. Rhonny would go back to Florida, Bif would dive back into her workaholic frenzy in Portland, and I would stay here on the island with the knowledge that my sisters thought I was a good mom for Mariah and with the peace of mind that I would always have their help and support.

I waved good-bye to my sisters the next morning from the dock as they departed on the mail boat knowing how lucky I was to be one of the three of us. It was unusual that the three of us had shared time alone. Their visit bolstered my confidence that Mariah and I would be fine, and it fortified my resolve to figure out my relationships in general. I was lucky. And, more important, Mariah was lucky.

I arrived home to a new message on my answering machine. The caller ID indicated Evergreen Academy. I wondered what today's ailment was and what pharmaceutical would be recommended. It wasn't a nurse this time. It was an administrator. Mariah was in real trouble and in danger of expulsion.

CHAPTER 11

Fight for It

I prepared to return the call to Evergreen with an attitude. Really? What had Mariah done now that was *so* awful that it might cost her the privilege of a private school education? Had she had the gall once again to allow a boy to enter her dorm room? Had she been brazen enough to leave school without permission to walk to Dunkin' Donuts? Had she slept through muster, or whatever they called the early morning attendance requirement? Had she hatefully eaten something that didn't belong to her from the group refrigerator? Had she skipped class? Oh, it must be another dress code violation—Mariah liked to make a statement, not so much a fashion statement as a thumbing of her nose at the overly strict policy. For God's sake, the kid is a kid, I thought as I prepared to refuse to go get her for such minor violations of what I had come to regard as militant rule. And so close to the end of the school year! They simply can't kick her out. At times we mothers have to defend our children!

I had resisted, until now, any tendency to sympathize with Mariah when she complained of the strictness and pettiness of some of the school rules. I had been the total opposite at her age. I had loved school and everything about it. My mother had to fight me to stay home when I was sick because I hated to miss a day. I never thought that Evergreen had a conspiracy against Mariah and, of course, I understood that her attitude about it was absolutely typical of a kid her age who seemed a bit rebellious in a harmless way. But now that I had made a decision to be her mother figure, and had admitted to myself that mothering her would be best for us both, I knew the role included knowing when to fight *for* her rather than fighting her. Evergreen needed to cut my kid some slack. Home with me was not an option. She wanted and deserved this education, and I would fight for it.

But when I actually got on the phone with them, my wrath dissolved like lard in a skillet. I don't think I would have been surprised to learn that Mariah had been caught sharing a can of beer with her girlfriends. But it was like a kick in the chest to hear that she had gotten a half gallon of whiskey in the mail. The package, which Mariah had apparently been looking for and asking about daily, was bobbled by the school's mail clerk and smashed into reeking seriousness. The administration had a zero-tolerance policy, and Mariah was already on probation for violating the no-boys-in-girls'-rooms rule. (Her boyfriend, Liam, whom I liked in spite of my dislike of their status, had "accidentally" fallen asleep in Mariah's bed.) The administration was trying to get to the bottom of the booze situation, with little help from my tight-lipped kid. She would take the rap rather than rat out any accomplice. Yeah, right. Bullshit, I thought. If Mariah was going down, I would ensure that it would not be alone. We mothers have a responsibility to seek justice for our kids. I agreed, at the insistence of the school administrator, that I would get to Evergreen as soon as possible. They would have her pack up her things. I would, of course, bring her kicking and screaming home, where she would have more supervision. I understood that hard alcohol was an activity well beyond what the school was willing to take responsibility for. Mariah would soon be officially back to being my problem.

My next and immediate call was to Mariah, who did not pick up. Probably busy packing—or mixing cocktails, I thought angrily. Mariah had told the school administrator only that the booze had been sent by a friend, and that she had no idea what the package contained. The "friend" had told Mariah to be looking for a present. The "friend" was obviously not too bright as she had included her name, Brianna Wilson, and a return address on the package, which she had sent via the U.S. Postal Service. I dialed again. And again. And I kept dialing until I wore her down. She repeated her party line without wavering through my interrogation. "Let me get this straight," I said. "You were sent a bottle of whiskey by a friend of yours in Memphis. And you do not have a phone number for this friend?" This was met with some mumbling and sniffling. "Really? You have a friend who is close enough to send you a gift, but you have no way of getting in touch with her?" More mumbling, which I felt signified untruths. "You are a terrible liar, Mariah. I will find Brianna and thank her for what she has done for you. And I will be in your dorm room tomorrow at noon. Be there!" I hung up and realized that this was the first time in quite a while that I had had a conversation with Mariah in which she had not asked for anything, not a dog, not a prescription, not even forgiveness. I was fuming. I guess I never realized how much being lied to could hurt. Mariah's future was on the line. That was upsetting. Mariah was at the very least *contemplating* drinking whiskey. That sickened me. Being a mother isn't easy.

I worked quickly, suspecting that Mariah would be on the phone giving Brianna a heads-up. Now an expert on shutting off her phone service, I did so. That would piss off Mariah. I knew that she had other ways to communicate, but texting was her lifeline to her world. I would make it difficult for her to cover her tracks. I searched my phone's history of caller IDs, looking for any 812 area code that would lead me to Tennessee. Although I usually avoided speaking with Mariah's mother, she did make an occasional attempt to communicate. I scrolled down through the list of numbers until I found one that started with the dreaded 812. Mariah's mother answered. "I don't know if you are aware of what is going on, but Mariah is in trouble at school," I began.

"Well, she called me this morning, but I was busy and couldn't talk. I told her I would call back, but when I did it seemed her phone isn't working. Again." This woman's tone of voice bothered me. It was downtrodden and complaint ridden. And I had grown to dislike her accent, which amplified the whining tone. Call me a Yankee, but there's a fine line between a southern drawl and a whimper. And nearly everything she said was preceded or followed by a blessing of someone's heart. I didn't bother explaining what Mariah's trouble was. I asked if the mother knew Brianna Wilson. "No, that name doesn't mean anything to me." I asked her to do some research and find a phone number for me. "Well, I'll try." I insisted that I needed the information and urged her to put forth some effort. She promised to call me if she was able to turn up anything. It felt sort of icky teaming up with this woman whom I had previously classified as a loser. But I had a purpose, and that was more important than any standards I might have. (I do have standards—they are low, but I have them.) I was compelled to learn the truth. We mothers have to be part sleuth, I realized.

I waited for the phone to ring from 812 all night. It never did, leading me to believe that Brianna Wilson was a made-up name, and I suspected that the return address was bogus, too. The package had been postmarked from Memphis, but that was the only real evidence I had. I would need Mariah to squeal if I was to ever learn the truth. Yes, the booze had no doubt been sent from a friend who was also a minor. But somewhere along the sleazy chain an adult had to have purchased the whiskey. I wanted to know who. But, I surmised, some kid could have stolen the jug from parents unbeknownst to them. Exasperated, I squirmed in bed until daylight searching for comfort that seemed frustratingly just beyond my reach. In times like these, we mothers lose a lot of sleep, I realized.

The few people with whom I shared the morning mail boat asked where I was off to. I fumbled around with an answer that would not divulge anything. I was embarrassed to think that

Mariah was being expelled from school for such poor judgment. I never thought her actions would have any effect on me, but I was wrong. I was taking some ownership of her, for sure. But when I returned with Mariah—bags and all—our friends would have to be told. And soon the entire island would know and be equally disappointed in her. But it was her story to tell at this point, not mine. Again, I wasn't sure what I was protecting, and whether what needed protecting was mine, hers, or ours. I am a true heart-on-sleever, so my face was surely less than poker. I stuck my head into the newspaper that was folded open to the daily crossword puzzle and attempted to finish what someone else had started. It's never much fun to jump into a puzzle someone else has given up on. All of the easy clues are filled in, leaving the ones that are impossible. On the other hand, you do feel pretty smart when you get a word or two that the last guy couldn't. The problem is, the last guy might have made some mistakes, totally throwing off your chances of satisfactory completion. And the puzzle solvers who use ink pens create a real mess for the next person, who might want to make corrections. When I realized that Mariah had a lot in common with the puzzle, I put it down and stared out the window until the boat kissed the dock.

Three hours later, I was pulling into Norway, Maine. It was a stellar day. The sun shined brightly on the snow-capped White Mountains that appeared to hem Evergreen Academy's western campus, cupping the lush, liquidlike grounds. Stark, masculine brick buildings supported by strong, white pillars were like islands emerging from giant green puddles. I parked in front of Eustis Hall, within which Mariah lived under a steeple and viewed the world outside through arched windows that must soften the sight of even the most wicked weather. A boy on a skateboard pumped past me, dipping one leg oarlike into pristine blacktop. The athletic field below the dormitory had a scattering of kids cradling lacrosse sticks and seemingly loving just being outside. Scholars with books under arms and packs on backs hustled purposefully between buildings. These young people are so lucky, I thought. This school had so much to offer. The enrichment courses beyond harsh academics were extraordinary. Mariah had learned silversmithing this year and was involved in a farm and forest program that was second to none; there was actually a working farm right on campus. She was enrolled in an academic skills program where she could get one-on-one tutoring in any subject. Her grades were lukewarm but improving. I have never thought that grades are a true indication of what value a student is gaining from education. As long as Mariah was putting forth her best effort and behaving, I had no complaints. How could Mariah have blown this opportunity? Mothering is frustrating.

I gave one knock on Mariah's dorm room door and entered. Mariah sat crossed-legged on the floor crying, surrounded by half-packed boxes and duffel bags. Her roommate was sitting on the edge of her bed, there for what I assumed was moral support. Mariah looked as though she had not slept. It didn't appear that lying was treating her very well. "I am only going to ask this once. You'll have to live with the answer for a long time," I said. "Who sent the booze?"

"My mother." Honesty this brutal sucked the life out of the room and left a silence so pronounced that I thought I heard the tears as they streamed down Mariah's agony-filled face. This was so far from what I had expected to hear that I was stunned and at a loss for what to say. My anger with Mariah quickly morphed into pity. There was no sense berating her mother, was there? It must now be quite clear without my rubbing her nose in it, I thought. "She begged me not to tell." I'll bet she did, I thought to myself. Sending a half gallon of whiskey to your daughter and asking her to take the full brunt of the consequences when the scheme went amok spoke volumes about Mom's makeup. Not that I didn't already have a pretty good read of her. "And now I'm going to be kicked out of school." More tears and uncontrollable sobbing . . .

"Get yourself together. We have a meeting with the assistant head of school in ten minutes," I said sternly. "Do you want to go home with me or do you want to finish the school year here?" Mariah stated between gasps for breath that she wanted to remain at Evergreen but that she would no doubt be expelled for this most recent stunt because she was already on probation. "Get a grip. Let's go. I am on your side at this meeting as long as you tell the truth." Even though I felt like choking Mariah, we mothers have to be united with our daughters in fights like the one I anticipated.

The walk across campus was long and quiet. Every student we passed gave Mariah a knowing look, and I sensed a shared grief for her troubles. Evergreen, like Isle au Haut, is a small, close community. Word had spread quickly.

I held the door, forcing Mariah to enter the assistant dean's office ahead of me. Eleanor Pratt was a nice woman who had been very supportive of my work to get Mariah back to Evergreen after her former guardian had pulled the plug. Now Eleanor was in the awkward position of enforcing a rule that would expel the one student who would perhaps benefit most from being at Evergreen. Mariah and I sat in wooden chairs across the desk from the assistant dean. After a warm greeting between Eleanor and me, Mariah spoke nervously. "I am sorry I lied to you both. Mrs. Pratt, my mother sent me the whiskey. It was stupid. And I am sorry." After Eleanor Pratt got over the shock of what she had been told, she explained that a disciplinary hearing would tell the fate of Mariah, and that the meeting was scheduled for the next day. She thanked Mariah for coming clean but reminded her that because she was already on probation, there was little hope that she would be allowed to finish the year. Mariah and I both acknowledged that we understood the situation.

"Should you be in class?" I asked Mariah.

"Math. But what's the point?"

"You haven't been expelled yet. Get to class and I'll talk to you later." Mariah hurried out of the office relieved and, I assume, confused, leaving Eleanor and me alone to hash things over.

"I have been at Evergreen for a very long time. I thought I had seen it all. Wow." Eleanor is a genuinely caring person for all of her students, but had special warmth for Mariah, I thought. "I am sorry that there is no way around this."

"Technically, Mariah never had the booze in her possession," I said suddenly. "My understanding is that the bottle was broken by the mail room clerk before Mariah picked it up." I thought for a minute before continuing. "And I am not hanging around here until tomorrow for the disciplinary board to do the right thing, which I am confident it will." Eleanor sat quietly, nodding her head in what I thought could have been agreement. "If the disciplinary board wants to press charges against Mariah's mother, I'll gladly come back to collect my kid, as it is clear to me that she solicited the booze shipment and then lied. But if her mother is not held accountable, Mariah should not be punished." Eleanor promised to pass all of this along to the board and to call me with their decision. We mothers have to be part attorney, I decided.

It felt strange leaving the campus and Mariah behind, knowing that it was quite likely that I would return the following day. But I knew some windshield time would do me more good than sitting in a hotel room in Norway, Maine, waiting for some faceless group to decide Mariah's and my fate. And leaving showed that my words were more than words. Unless Evergreen pressed charges against Mariah's mother, she would remain a student in good standing (on probation, of course). As I drove out of town, it struck me what a strange place this school actually was. The staunchly bricked and pillared and quaint New England Main Street lined with trendy, independent coffee shops boasting of organic and fair-trade wares and free Wi-Fi was juxtaposed with modest homes, a gas station with simple hot coffee, and a drab public school. As Ivy League preparatory disappeared in my rearview mirror and the school of hard knocks sprawled ahead, I believed that Mariah represented a poignant connection between the haves and have-nots. And I prayed that the disciplinary board would see the value in her presence as a bridge over that tremendous gap.

The argument about nature versus nurture has remained unresolved for a very long time, so it was unlikely I would figure it out in a four-hour commute. Sadly, whichever side of the equation I favored, to my mind Mariah didn't stand a chance. If her mother was indicative, nature did not bode well. And if nurture began at birth, the scenario was bleak for the same reason. So her mother plays the lead role in either nature or nurture. How discouraging. I wondered if I was being unfair or too severe regarding her biological mom. I wondered what her mother's situation was and how her rearing had shaped her. I wondered about the perpetual cycles of abuse I had heard about. But that wonder only existed for a second because it all seemed so hopeless, so glass half empty.

I thought it must be hard for Mariah to have one foot rooted in her own family's traditions and the other tentatively toeing the ground of better opportunity. I wondered whether straddling was a conscious choice. She had nominated me as her guardian in a legal procedure. But other than that single signature on a single document at a moment when she was confused and traumatized, Mariah hadn't been given much in the way of choices. Or perhaps she had been asked to make too many choices. Perhaps expecting her to choose was expecting too much. Mariah needed more than a guardian. She needed remedial nurturing and someone to be responsible for choices beyond food and clothing. She needed help making life choices. And it was at that moment that I vowed to choose for her. No matter how Evergreen's disciplinary board ruled, for better or for worse, I would decide for Mariah until I felt she was capable of doing so herself. Isn't that what my mother had done for me?

CHAPTER 12

Change Was Good

I can't say that I was surprised to hear that Evergreen's disciplinary board had decided that another chance was in order for Mariah. Relieved is more like it. Eleanor Pratt made it clear that this was a highly unusual case and that they were making an extraordinary exception by allowing Mariah to remain in school—on probation, of course, for another year. I suspected, even with all that Eleanor had said about how special Mariah was and how the school wanted to do its part appropriately in her well-being and education, that the board had wisely chosen not to test the ultimatum I had left on its doorstep about my kid. I would like to think that Evergreen was sincere in wanting to do the right thing, but I realized that the right thing might well have been to give Mariah the boot as dictated by the school's rules and the penalties for breaking them.

I truly believed that Mariah's mother should be held accountable. For the briefest moment I wondered what their decision and seeming unwillingness to prosecute the responsible adult was teaching my kid about following rules and suffering consequences. But I just as quickly justified Mariah's remaining in school as the most valuable outcome regardless of any deep-seated morals that may be conflicted. This situation flew in the face of my deeply held convictions about personal responsibility and accountability. If it had been Mariah's roommate whose head was on the chopping block, would I feel the same? And just to drive the point home about the tentative relationship between behavior and consequences, I turned Mariah's phone back on (even though I had threatened never to do so) so that I could call and let her know what was what.

Mariah had gotten off on a technicality. My mother might have been right when she told me that I should have become an attorney. More poignant was the fact that this was the first time I had stood up for Mariah in a motherly way. And that felt good.

"Hello?"

"Hi. It's Linny. They decided to let you stay and finish the year."

"I'm flunking algebra . . . yet again."

"I'll hire another tutor. You'll have to take a summer course."

"Oh, that sounds like fun!" Her sarcasm bothered me.

"Forget about fun. You are on probation for another year. You can't afford even a minor offense."

"I'll be good. I promise. Thanks, Linny." And that was the first and only time that Mariah had ever promised me anything, and come to think of it, the first time she had thanked me out of something other than direct obligation. Although I was touched by her sincerity, I was still nervous that she might misbehave before I picked her up on the Saturday following final exams to go home for the summer. But she did not. I heard no more from the school, and she jumped right into two jobs when her feet hit the island, then landed a third job on Sundays manning the island's only gift shop. I hired a beautiful, young island woman, Morgan, to tutor Mariah through an online algebra course that she desperately needed to pass to become a high school junior. Mariah connected with Morgan and I couldn't have been happier about that. It was good for Mariah to have nearly daily contact with someone of Morgan's quality. Not only did Morgan coach Mariah into a passing grade, but she was also a great influence and inspiring role model in many other ways. Imagine somebody cool and hip who loves math! Amazing, indeed.

Logistics are more of a task than the task itself here on the island, and life had been complicated before I introduced a teenager's schedule into the mix. I was already not caring much for carting Mariah everywhere she needed to be. Oh, she drove on the island without a license like everybody else, but every time she had an appointment, social engagement, or an urge to shop on the mainland, it gobbled up a full day of my life. But, as they say, where there is a will there is a way. It was time for Mariah to get her driver's license, so I started researching where, when, and how. I found a highly regarded program right in Stonington, which did mean I'd have to take her ashore for class and driving lessons two nights a week, but the payoff would be good. Even more incentive to get that license! When I learned that Mariah needed to show a birth certificate to enroll in the class, I knew I didn't have a copy. Neither did she. Not to worry, though. I got on the Internet and found the number for vital statistics in Tennessee. I told the nice man what I needed. He asked for Mariah's date and place of birth. I gave them to him, ordered two copies, and gave him my credit card info. So easy!

Not so easy. The nice man phoned the next day to report that he had no record of Mariah's birth on that date at that location. Did I have the correct date, he asked? Was I certain she was born in Memphis, Tennessee? Could she possibly have been born in another state? How would I know? I knew only what Mariah believed and what had been unquestioned until now. Did she have another name, he asked? There was no way I could ask Mariah if there was a chance that she had no idea who she was or where she was born or how old she was. She loved her birthday and had started a countdown months before, sending me daily reminders. I needed to confirm what she thought she knew, not let on that she might not have a clue as to her beginnings or identity. And I needed a birth certificate pronto!

So I did what any resourceful, slightly desperate mother would do under the circumstances. I got online again and found a sleazy site that promised official-looking documents. Two days and more money than I care to admit later, Mariah was Mariah and she was born on her birthday in her birthplace. Cool! I assumed that the name, place, and date of birth that Mariah had lived with was indeed accurate, and now we had the paperwork to back it up. I wondered if my Web activity and purchase of a birth certificate that might be phony would come back to haunt Mariah later in life. In the end I decided that it wasn't worth mentioning. So what if she wasn't born on the exact date she had celebrated every year. Lots of people manipulate birthdays to accommodate schedules. My own birthday is so close to Christmas that my family often acknowledges it on the twenty-fifth, when we are all together. (Not a highly religious holiday for the Greenlaws, and I never thought Jesus Christ was stealing my thunder as so many people have voiced concern about through the years when they learn of my birth date.) Anyway, my powers of justifying my possibly seedy actions were in overdrive. (Oddly enough, Mariah did come with a Social Security card. Goes to show you the diligence of Uncle Sam when potential taxes are at risk.)

I couldn't help but notice that a driver's license was not at the top of Mariah's priority list, which confused me slightly. I saw this as a necessary and natural step toward independence and maturity. I recalled getting my own license and how eager I was to do so. And even though I was perhaps a bit selfish in wanting Mariah to have hers to free up my personal schedule, I remembered my mother doing the same thing for the same reason. Every time I asked to use the family car (which was daily) when I was a teen driver, the answer was "Yes. Take the kids." So virtually everywhere I went at the age of fifteen, I had the seven-year-old twins in tow. This was fine when it was a basketball game or ice-cream run, but I had to put my foot down when it was time for high school dances. I thought all teens were dying to get their licenses. This was not the case with Mariah. Maybe independence and maturity were things I wanted for her and that she was not ready for. She went along with the idea easily enough, though. And we began our two nights off island each week for ten weeks.

Somewhat to my surprise, instead of adding to my own resentment, we both quickly began to look forward to our nights off including boat rides on the *Mattie Belle*. Mariah had always had a special fondness for the boat, and had even named one of her hamsters Mattie Belle when she first arrived on island. The ride over to driver's ed gave us some great regular time for plain ol' catching up because we didn't see each other that much during the rest of the week with our work schedules and diametrically opposed sleep routines. I would drop Mariah off at the school and then do some grocery shopping, filling the car with items from her list and mine. After class we would go out to dinner at a restaurant right on the water from where we could see the *Mattie Belle* at the public dock. The ride home well after dark was comfortable and silent.

One night at dinner after driver's ed I asked Mariah how her job at the Inn at Isle au Haut was going. She said that she liked the job, although it was hard work. She loved being around the sole proprietor, Diana, and all of the gourmet food she prepared for her guests. Mariah had the luck to be fed dinner at the inn each night that she worked that shift, and was proud to tell me that she tried many things she had never before eaten, and really enjoyed them. Then she hesitated and frowned. "What?" I asked.

"Well, no offense," Mariah began. "But it is annoying when the guests question me about why I live with you."

Diana had warned me that her guests love to chitchat with

the island people and that Mariah would be questioned about where she lived and what her parents do, et cetera. "That doesn't offend me. It is nearly impossible to offend me. And that is *not* a challenge," I laughed. "What do you tell them?" I asked curiously.

"At first I would just get embarrassed and run for the kitchen. But last night this woman wouldn't leave me alone. She kept firing questions at me. Once she learned that I live with the *famous* Linda Greenlaw, she wouldn't let it go until she understood *why* that was so and what it was *like* to live with you."

"It's your story to tell. Tell what you want to whom you want, and nothing more," I said, repeating the advice that I had shared so many times with her. "So, what *did* you tell her?"

Mariah hesitated, and then shrugged. "I told her that I was in need of some major nagging and that you needed a pain in your ass, and that both of our needs are being met." Mariah looked cautious, as if she might have crossed a line.

I raised my glass of wine to clink against her milk and said, "Touché! Now for confession time: When people ask where the hell you came from, I tell them the stork left you on my doorstep when you were fifteen."

"Linny!" We both started to laugh a much needed laugh.

"Well, I guess we both have our own ways of avoiding the whole gory story," I said.

"It is pretty gory, isn't it?"

"Oh yeah. But you know what the best part is? The best part is that we can talk about it in the past tense." Mariah agreed for the most part, but confided, after looking over her shoulder and lowering her voice, that she was still afraid that Ken would be found not guilty and would get out of jail. I promised Mariah that he would never bother her again. "He will never step foot on our island." She said that she wasn't scared for herself. She was worried that he would find another victim.

I learned a lot about Mariah at that table that night. And I was proud and unhesitant with my introductions of her simply as "Mariah." No other explanation was needed as far as I could see.

Daily routines were one thing, but there was a big moment looming: the resolution of the case against Ken. We were on a wild emotional roller coaster together, united by our hopes and fears of the possible outcome. The court had assigned Mariah a victim's advocate (a real title and one that I would not use otherwise, because Mariah *never* let on that she was a victim), and she kept us in the loop about upcoming hearings (putting us on edge), continuances and postponements (frustrating!), and failure after failure for the court-appointed defending attorney as he painstakingly exhausted each avenue available to his client. After each one we'd exhale and sink back in our seats.

Change was good, and we underwent many changes during that summer. I had the basement finished with a bedroom and bathroom for Mariah, allowing her to move out of what we still called the guest bedroom. I noticed that Mariah began referring to the house as "ours," and I no longer had to wonder whether her "home" was Maine or Tennessee. I no longer felt that Mariah interrupted my life; instead, I knew that she enriched my life. Now when I would say no to some of Mariah's requests, she responded with easy acceptance. There was no begging or pleading when the answer was no. Indeed, she seemed happy to be forbidden to do certain things. In the past when I had friends in for social time, Mariah would revert to coloring books and crayons. Now she joined the conversation and no longer complained of being with "old people" all the time. Mariah was becoming quite a socially adept young woman whom my friends enjoyed. Life fell into a comfortable normalcy. And I no longer questioned whether I should go fishing or not. I knew it was all right for me to continue along my chosen path, which Mariah would take in stride. Our very separate lives synced smoothly. She did her thing. I did my thing. And when we were together, we did our thing.

I left on a fishing trip before Mariah started school again that fall, leaving her in good hands. Bif took over as guardian and mother figure, doing the school prep shopping, transporting, and advising. Mariah moved in with Bif and her husband, Ben, in their year-round home in Harpswell, Maine. When Mariah complained of homesickness, Bif was kind enough to collect her from school and take her home for a weekend in Harpswell, where she got lots of coddling from Aunt Bif and great food prepared by Uncle Ben. When I called and informed Mariah that I had been arrested and put in a Canadian jail for fishing violations, Bif let me know that Mariah was fine with this information. Bif attended all court proceedings and hearings on my behalf as they pertained to Ken and his pending trial. I fished the Grand Banks season without a worry about how Mariah was doing in my absence. At the end of my fishing season, when I picked her up for her Thanksgiving break, I hadn't seen Mariah in three months.

She looked great. She was happy. Her grades had improved slightly. She appeared to have come into her own and was thriving in a way that I hadn't witnessed before. And we shared the excitement and anticipation of going home to a place we both loved knowing that neither of us had been there since we'd left together, me to the Grand Banks and Mariah to Evergreen.

I also stepped into the new role as family grown-up and began making unilateral decisions about what was right and wrong for Mariah. Real parents don't always consult their kids, especially about thorny emotional issues. When Christmas rolled around and Mariah was torn about whether to go to Tennessee or not, I decided that she would stay home—with me. We sent gifts for her brothers, mother, and aunt and went to Florida for two weeks. (My older sister, Rhonda, had Mariah the first week in Florida—absolutely spoiling her rotten—while I worked to meet a deadline.) On spring break I took Mariah on her first visit to New York City, where we went to see *The Lion King* on Broadway. We ate at fine restaurants, met up with dear friends, and wandered Macy's looking for dresses for formal dinners at school. Her only complaint was that the trip was too short.

Yes, life was good. Mariah entered her senior year at Evergreen Academy no longer on probation. I was not nervous that she would do anything to jeopardize her diploma. She worked with a guidance counselor to apply to colleges, and seemed surprised to be doing so. She confided that she didn't know of anyone in her biological family who had attended college and that not many had finished high school, a signal to me of the many things I had taken for granted. Bif took Mariah to visit colleges in the Boston area. Simon drove her to check out some schools in Vermont. Mariah told me that her group of friends graduating with her from Evergreen were all going to Colorado, some to study and some to live and hang out. I suspected that she might prefer the hanging out to attending college and told her to forget it. Among this group of Colorado-bound kids was Mariah's boyfriend, with whom she had been connected at the hip since her sophomore year. "Not happening!" I had first met Liam when Mariah and I were visiting Evergreen just prior to her reacceptance. He had followed us around campus like a lost puppy, and had been part of the picture ever since. A total dichotomy in my view, Liam was a high-achieving slacker. A wrestling champ and straight A student who didn't need to hit the books, Liam was a bit of a Daddy's little rich kid. I had indications from things that Mariah told me that Liam's parents did not approve of the relationship either. As relieved as I was to understand that Mariah was at least in a monogamous relationship, my observations were that Liam didn't treat Mariah with much respect. Hadn't he been partly responsible for her probation by being caught in her room? So postponing college to hang out with him was not optimum.

Mariah inquired about the possibility of doing a gap year program. "If it is a program that colleges will accept as worthy of a year of your time before entering college, fine. If not, forget about it." When Mariah delved into acceptable programs, she quickly leaned back in the direction of traditional college matriculation with a freshman class.

Mariah's first choice was Ethan Allen College in Vermont. Her guidance counselor told me that it was a stretch but that she didn't want to discourage Mariah from applying because she wasn't showing a lot of enthusiasm for other schools. I spoke with Mariah about what I saw as fear in her. I said that it was natural that she would be scared at this major juncture in her life—everyone is! I told her about my experience at Colby College and even got a little sentimental when relaying the fact that I begged my parents to take me back home before the car was unloaded. I urged Mariah to apply and pushed her to check into scholarship possibilities. The counselor at Evergreen helped Mariah through the FAFSA (Free Application for Federal Student Aid) process, filing as an independent as I had not adopted her. All of this was like pulling teeth. Mariah became very moody, and it seemed to me that she had taken a few steps backward emotionally. She was as confused as could be, pulling away from me and putting up the old barriers. She even started some really childlike behavior: The coloring books came out.

She was keen enough to go to college, but it seemed she wasn't so hot on the real commitment it was going to take. Here was one place where my sympathy dried up fast. When Mariah complained that she didn't want to borrow money for school, I said, "Tough. Everyone does. Suck it up." I explained that I had fished my way through college, working on the deck of a sword boat. And I still had to borrow money. I'm sure all of that sounded like the barefoot-uphill-to-school lecture. I was aware of the possibility that Mariah might have assumed I would foot her entire four-year college tab. I agreed to contribute what I could as long as she did her part by working and borrowing and scholarship searching. When speaking to the financial aid folks at various schools,

I always needed to explain that Mariah was not my birth child. I hadn't had eighteen years to plan and save for her education. I sort of felt that I was on the defensive when justifying why my kid was an independent with regard to any aid packages.

When she was accepted at Ethan Allen, there was no backing out. She had miraculously gotten into her school of choice against great odds. But after the initial thrill of achievement of acceptance, she became quite negative. She began talking about Colorado with a longing, and being cheated out of something that others had, and sort of whining about *having* to go to college. I explained that she certainly did not *have* to go. But if she chose not to go, she had better plan on getting a job. There was no suitable year-round employment on Isle au Haut. I absolutely forbade her to stay on Isle au Haut and do nothing like so many others before her. The tension that had eased in our relationship was piano-string tight once again. Our phone calls were few, brief, and unpleasant. During these calls, I could tell that something was weighing heavily; I assumed the fear of college. Once again I began questioning my decision to bring this girl into my otherwise happy life.

I voiced my sadness to Bif, who had an interesting and, I now think, quite accurate insight. "She turns eighteen in two weeks and graduates from high school the following week. Mariah is acutely aware that your legal guardianship terminates automatically on her eighteenth birthday. She must think you'll be done with her like every other parental figure she's had. Right?" I didn't comprehend the depth and breadth of what Bif suggested until much later. For all our comfort and closeness of late, secretly a part of me wished I *could* be done that easily. The better part of me, though, knew that this was a long-term relationship and that as the grown-up, I had to find a way to ease Mariah's fears. "You'll just have to let the brat know that she's stuck with us!" Bif teased. I wondered how I would do that while we barely spoke and when we did, Mariah was so bitchy I felt like slapping her. Who is stuck with whom? What did stick was the nickname. Mariah officially and affectionately became "the brat."

When the caller ID on my home phone read "U.S. Government," I was not alarmed because I had become accustomed to Mariah's court advocate calling with updates that were later received via the post office. When I learned that Ken had pleaded guilty to both charges of which he had been accused—possession and transportation of child pornography—I was hugely relieved. Ken was now awaiting sentencing. This news was well beyond welcome. It was joyous because we now understood that Mariah would not have to testify in court. She had the option of speaking or reading a statement at the sentencing, the very thought of which threw her a huge emotional fastball. Our own relationship, only recently realigned, now teetered on a knife's edge.

Mariah wanted to appear and face Ken if doing so would amount to a stricter sentence, she said. But neither the federal prosecutor nor her advocate could tell her whether her showing up would have any effect or influence on the outcome. I couldn't help but think that seeing Ken would inevitably set off mixed and strong emotions in Mariah. Ken had been Mariah's only caregiver for several years. He had been responsible for moving her to the island, which, admittedly, might ultimately have saved her life. I felt that Mariah would not benefit from seeing Ken, and I wanted to protect her from another unintended consequence: In some emotionally laden twist of logic, she might be haunted by the idea that she had contributed to his demise (leaving aside the fact that half the island population would happily have done just that, literally). Mariah must surely have a tender spot in her heart for her abuser. Although she had never shown or verbalized anything that hinted at the Stockholm syndrome, I knew that it was a survival strategy. And Mariah was certainly a survivor.

After several days of discussion and flip-flopping on the topic, I made the decision that Mariah would not attend the sentencing. "You are not going. You need to stay at school and not worry about it. I'll go and speak on your behalf and will call you immediately afterward." And that was that.

The days leading up to the sentencing, graduation, and Mariah's plunge into legal adulthood were dreadful: Three huge life cycle events converged in one short period. The calls back and forth had virtually come to an end. Mariah wasn't even calling to get permission to leave campus, something she had been doing like clockwork. The daily reminders and countdown of days to her birthday stopped. She didn't even e-mail me asking for a bit of spending money. She did submit a written statement to the judge who would preside at the sentencing procedure. I wouldn't have known that, but her advocate sent me a copy to read so that I could better ready my statement. Mariah's written testimony was eloquent, succinct, and mature. I called to say that she had done a great job with it, and ended up leaving a message that was never returned.

I didn't know how I would feel about laying eyes on Ken

knowing the lengths to which he had gone to ruin another human being's life—and a child's at that. In my opinion, he had not quite succeeded. But the jury was still out on that, so to speak. I braced myself psychologically for what I might feel at the sight of him. Would I feel sickened? Would I be frightened? Would I be enraged? I was as nervous as a cat as I sat and waited impatiently on the hard, cold bench in the federal courtroom in Portland. When Ken was led in locked in handcuffs, I went numb, and for an instant felt removed from the scene. I quickly reentered, and thought how pathetic he looked, and I felt sorry for him. Bif and Simon flanked me, providing much needed support through the legal jargon and pomp and circumstance of robes, suits, and ties, which seemed too ill fitting at this particular occasion to determine the fate of a man so pale and bloated that he appeared to have been stuffed into his orange jumpsuit.

The proceedings seemed to crawl in waves, like a tide that would surge ahead two inches and then recede and regroup before making another attempt to come ashore. There were motions heard from both the defending attorney and the government's, one asking the judge to impose a sentence in the lower range of the guidelines, and the other requesting a departure upward from the range. There was a question as to the authenticity of Mariah's written statement, to which I testified that it was indeed hers. Both attorneys presented their cases regarding the appropriate sentence. And finally, witnesses were asked to speak. I was the only witness.

As I was sworn in, my voice cracked and I was afraid that I would melt down as I had in front of my community so many months, tears, laughs, triumphs, failures, and days of frustrating anguish before. I was asked before I began to please avoid the use of names. Because Mariah was a minor, I should refer to her as "MJ" or "my legal ward."

My name is Linda Greenlaw and I'm here on behalf of some of the victims in this case, primarily a young girl whom I will refer to as my daughter, because that is what she has become. Although I'm sure Your Honor understands that MJ is not my biological daughter, according to the state of Maine, I am her legal guardian. Prior to guardianship, I had what I would consider limited involvement and contact with MJ.

Limited contact and involvement is a pretty relative term. We live on a small island where there is a year-round population of about fifty people, so the involvement and contact in a small island is much deeper and more frequent than you would see in a big city.

Around half a dozen years or so ago, the defendant moved to the island from Memphis and was soon followed by this little girl he referred to as his niece. His story was that he was saving his niece from a very bad family situation, including a heroin junkie stepfather, extreme poverty, abuse, and a half-wit mother who, it appeared, had virtually given her daughter away.

We love our children on my island. We value family. The community accepted with open arms the defendant and his niece. The defendant was thought a hero for saving this beautiful little girl. Fast-forward four years: The defendant got sloppy. An admitted alcoholic, he fell off the wagon in a big way, bringing to light the fact that he was not saving this little girl. He had, in fact, taken her from the frying pan into the fire. With all due respect to the defense, my entire community was duped by the defendant. I think the defense has been duped by his client regarding the question of intent. The defendant is an extremely clever pedophile who fooled an entire community. I can't ask or expect Your Honor to put yourself in the victim's shoes. Imagining the abuse she endured is beyond comprehension. The lengths to which the defendant went to destroy the life of an innocent child is unimaginable. He began grooming—and I do believe "grooming" is appropriate—his victim long before moving to Maine. They shared a bed every weekend for at least three years in Memphis, Tennessee.

I can't ask you to put yourself in the place of the victim, but I can ask you to try, if you will, to see this from my perspective. Imagine reprimanding a young girl about personal hygiene: MJ, you are thirteen years old, you need to bathe every day. You know, it's very important. Imagine how you would feel later when you learned about the hidden camera in the bathroom and the fact that she became aware that her trusted and loved guardian had been photographing and videotaping her while she bathed. The last year under the defendant's guardianship, MJ was taking her dry and clean clothes into the shower with her to change because she didn't know if the camera was on, or where it was. And she knew that it was connected directly to her uncle's computer. Imagine explaining to your daughter that the advice from public health to parents to talk about sex with their kids did not include show-and-tell. Does the advice to talk about sex with your kids give a guardian license to share details of his own sexual exploits and complaints of abstinence from certain sexual activities due to the extraordinary size of the penis?

Imagine explaining that driver's education at the age of fifteen does not require sitting in the instructor's lap. Imagine explaining to your daughter that the twelve-year-old boy Cody, who coerced her into taking and sending over the Internet naked pictures of herself, was actually a fabrication of her guardian and uncle, the defendant. As were the young girls from Texas who sent pictures of the defendant's penis to my daughter. As was Marie the defendant's self-manufactured French girlfriend and cybersex partner, complete with broken English.

The defendant fits the definition of the classic pedophile by his mind control and total manipulation of his prey. That's just the tip of the iceberg, and I won't go on because I'm sure you've heard plenty.

Last, imagine, if you can, explaining to this beautiful young lady why the defendant, her abuser, did not, if it happens today, receive the maximum sentence. What he did wasn't bad enough? That's a tough sell. He got brownie points for having no criminal record? He's just never been caught. The defendant did not wake up at the age of forty-six and decide he had sexual desires for young children.

What makes this case different from others? What makes this case different from others of sexual abuse and child pornography? I've been asking myself that question. Why should Your Honor consider a sentence upward rather than below the range? Most crimes and offenses of this nature are hidden and private. The defendant made this abuse public when he invited his victim's male peers to become voyeurs and abusers themselves. He sent my daughter's school friends pictures of her naked in a way that falsely indicated that she had sent them herself.

Imagine forming some compelling and reasonable argument to urge your daughter that she did, in fact, have to return to high school. Imagine convincing her that she has nothing to be ashamed of and that she can hold her head high above her school chums' voices calling her a "porn star." I hate what the defendant has done to my daughter. I hate what the defendant has done to my community. He has shattered our naïveté. We are riddled with guilt for not seeing the truth and, in fact, enabling the abuse.

I hate what the defendant has done to me personally. I now question the way I interact with the island children. Is it okay for me to hug Johnny or pat Alex or ruffle Andrew's hair? Is it okay for me to share a hotel room with my daughter? The eye-opening and stomach-turning truth about the defendant has made me paranoid and has profoundly changed the way I think and act. I understand that it is within my rights to seek financial restitution in this case. I have chosen not to do so. No amount of money will erase the years of abuse suffered by my daughter. Believe me, I'd love for her nightmares to go away. Money can't restore my community's innocence or ease our feelings of guilt. The best we can do is ask Your Honor for the maximum sentence. I consider the opportunity for this little bit of input today a real privilege and I thank you for hearing me.

Phew. I was sure the entire courtroom heard me exhale as I sat down between Bif and Simon. Bif squeezed my hand and Simon gave me a reassuring nod. Frankly, I was amazed that I had referred to Mariah as my daughter without planning to. It just came out, and seemed okay. Thank God she hadn't heard it, I thought. The hint of being my *anything* right now might trigger her oversensitive gag reflex or cause pain in her chest or bring on hives. Ken had his turn at the podium and, as I recall, was remorseful. I figured his attorney coached him on that. I didn't hear most of what he read from the single white sheet of paper that crinkled in his shaking hands. My mind was more on Mariah's birthday and how we'd celebrate it a few days late in conjunction with her graduation party and congrats-on-college-acceptance soiree. We'd do it up in true Greenlaw fashion, I thought. The judge left the courtroom for his chambers, leaving me in the caring hands of Bif and Simon.

The judge returned to the courtroom. We all rose. The judge asked us to be seated. The sentencing itself was far different from what I had imagined, and what I had imagined was inspired by my childhood television experience watching *Perry Mason*. I was impressed that the judge was so thoughtful. He explained everything in detail while I kept waiting for him to growl and come out with some number of years for Ken to be incarcerated and then slam down the gavel. There were "levels" added, which I figured were bad points for Ken. For example, there were two additional levels for material including prepubescent minors, five for distribution of child pornography to juveniles, four for images depicting violence against minors, and so on. And there were three levels subtracted for the defendant's accepting responsibility for his offenses, and that was the grand total of good points. The total offense level was thirty-seven and the criminal history was category one. This yielded a guideline range of 210 to 262 months. The judge sentenced Ken to 240 months on the trafficking offense and 120 months for possession. The judge noted that because it is impossible to traffic in child pornography without possessing it, the sentences were to be served concurrently. Bottom line: Ken was sentenced to 360 months, which was the maximum within the guideline range. When you added and subtracted all the pieces, he would be in jail for 240 months—20 years. That seemed like a good long time to me. Mariah would be safe.

I was eager to call Mariah and report that Ken had received the maximum sentence. I was disappointed once again to have to leave her a message, knowing that my call would not be returned. My sense of relief and satisfaction that justice had been served were shared by the island community. Once again my friends and family stepped up to join me in what could otherwise have been a very lonely feeling of strange triumph. I wished that Mariah would share that space with me, but maybe it was better that she didn't.

When I went to the post office I was surprised to have something in my box from Mariah. She had sent some tickets to her graduation and a note that read simply: "If anyone wants to come."

CHAPTER 13

A Mother Is Born

I n the spirit of "seeing is believing," and once again flanked by Simon and Bif, I gladly but somewhat skeptically took a seat among the hundreds of family members packed into a white tent that welcomed the proud parents of the pending graduates of Evergreen Academy. It was a steamy hot morning, the kind that finds everyone wiping a brow with the back of a hand. Nothing smells quite like dew evaporating from canvas. The aroma, as distinct as bacon, thickened the air in the same way. Graduation programs fanned perspiring necks and faces through the welcome address. Simon loosened his tie.

A small sea of white squares askew on heads and draping gowns in the front of the seating area shifted impatiently in metal folding chairs while a few nervous whispers escaped from under caps. I wasn't sure under which of the sixty squares Mariah sat.

They all looked alike from my perspective. And that was a good perspective in light of what I knew was so very different.

The awards part of the ceremony was long. There seemed to be endless lists of highest achieving students, Good Samaritans, and exceptional athletes, each called up one at a time. Each recipient of each scholarship made his or her way to the podium and shook hands with a right hand and grabbed a plaque and an envelope with the left while posing for posterity in a bright flash before exiting the stage and making way for the next smiling representative of wholesomeness. Have you ever watched a parade because you had to, one in which you were not genuinely interested? Float after float, marching bands, clowns on tricycles, majorettes, horses, the mayor's wife in a convertible . . . it was easy for me to drift away from the scene. Capped and gowned teenagers floated ghostlike across the platform, much like the sheep I was almost counting.

As the scholars and jocks cycled from and to their individual seats, so did the events littering my relationship with Mariah walk through my memory, where they'd gained their own pageantry. But I suppose that's what sentiment is, and what better time to allow myself a little human sentimentality. The only person in my entire life other than myself for whom I had taken responsibility had reached one of life's benchmarks. Mariah was graduating from high school! So much of what Mariah had achieved was not tangible or measurable to the human eye, so this diploma was a big deal. The fact that she was graduating from this fine school was equivalent to walking on the moon for a kid with a normal background. She had certainly come a long way.

I had come a long way. *We* had come a long, frustrating way. Had it really been three years since she'd arrived at my place—bag, baggage, and cat—for a short stay while her uncle got his act together? Wow. I wondered where we would go from here.

It was certainly her choice to stay within the nest or to take flight. It was her prerogative to call the place on Isle au Haut home or to leave it behind in search of whatever it is young people need. Because her eighteenth birthday had landed in the week of final exams, I hadn't seen her since she had been out from under my legal care. In our few conversations that consisted mostly of polite small talk, I spoke in terms that I believed gave her no choice other than to remain under my care and guardianship. Even if not legally bound to do so, I wanted to continue toward the goal of "us." Outwardly I wore my heart on my sleeve. I spoke nonchalantly and only in terms of "us" and "we" when discussing future options and plans. But I was secretly worried that she might not want my family, my friends, my house, or me.

While milling around the campus that morning before the ceremony, I met random parents of kids I had never met. Protocol dictated the same exchange over and over. "Who's your son or daughter? What does he or she have planned for the immediate future?" "Mariah" and "Ethan Allen," I bubbled naturally, happily, and yes, *proudly*. I'm not sure the words would have been as carefree if they had been spoken in Mariah's presence.

Beyond "Congratulations," I wondered what else I would say to Mariah after the ceremony. I shifted uncomfortably in my seat as Bif studied something on her phone and Simon gazed into space. What words of wisdom would I impart? What would a "real" mother say? I probably had another two hours or so to figure it out, I thought as I looked at the program and realized that Evergreen was still in the awards phase of the agenda. We still had to hear from the student speakers and to endure the commencement address before diplomas were dealt. I admired Mariah's name as it appeared in the list of graduates. Pretty official, I thought with a sigh. Suddenly my attention was torn from the program. What did I just hear? Bif reached out and tapped my knee rapidly and Simon applauded as Mariah made her way through the row of classmates and up the steps to the stage, where she was receiving an award. I clapped enthusiastically. When I turned to Bif with a look of question, she shrugged and laughed. "I was doing e-mail," she whispered apologetically. I turned to face Simon as he raised his eyebrows and shoulders simultaneously, indicating that he didn't know what Mariah was being recognized for either.

I didn't blink for fear of squeezing the tear that had pooled along my lower lid and sending it onto my cheek for all to see. I swallowed the tightness that gripped my throat. It didn't matter what Mariah had received an award for. She had been recognized. I sat taller in my chair and paid close attention to what remained of the commencement exercises. I was impressed with the students who took the podium to speak. The valedictorian asked his classmates to turn to one another and say "Good-bye," as that was something that hadn't been taught in the four years of private school education. Sure, they had had lots of practice with "See you later, See you after class, See you at the game, See you after break . . . ," but they had never had to say "Good-bye" to one another. And now it was time. I choked up again as I wondered how Mariah was handling that closing. She had some experience with hearing it. I wondered if she believed that she would never hear it from me.

The commencement speaker was actually a duo of father and son. They sucked. I thought that Evergreen Academy could have done better by this graduating class. This was such a big day! I suppose it wasn't so much what they said but more what they didn't say that I felt so profoundly lacking. This class needed to know how important their education was. They needed to be told that education could never be wasted—no matter what they chose to do with it. They needed to know that education is the one thing they had achieved that could never be taken away. I imagined that Mariah didn't care, so I decided to cut the speaking team some slack. Really, I thought, all this class *wants* to hear is "Congratulations!" I was worried because I knew some awkwardness was imminent as Mariah and I forged ahead.

After the last diploma was passed, the final applause had subsided, and the crowd dispersed from under the tent and sprawled out into the brilliant sunshine, Bif and Simon left for their homes. I found Mariah hugging friends and teachers and crying a few happy tears. She quickly handed me her diploma and award, and asked if I could carry them to the car for her. "What is the award for?" I asked.

"I have no idea! I wasn't paying attention either." Mariah laughed and was immediately swarmed by another group of friends wanting photos. "Can I meet you at the car? I won't be long." I agreed and told her to take her time. We were in no particular hurry. I experienced a mix of emotions as I walked Evergreen's campus for what I knew would be the last time. Mostly it was relief. I felt a slight twinge of sadness as I watched families posing for pictures around their new graduates.

Mariah, true to her word, was not long returning to the car. We worked together lugging boxes and bags of her belongings from her third-story dorm room to the Jeep. When the goldfish was placed in the only remaining open spot, we headed out in silence. I figured Mariah would curl up in a ball and fall asleep. But she didn't. She sat happily and alertly by my side and seemed to be comfortable in the quiet. Her phone rang. "Hello? Oh hi. Thank you. It was great! Hey, can I call you later? I'm in the car with my mom. We're heading home."

Afterword

As of this writing, I have achieved a new level of selfishness and have managed to disguise it as a generous act of kindness for Mariah. She just left to begin her sophomore year of college in a brand-new, shiny, jet-black, 2012 Volkswagen Jetta. Hey, I didn't feel like driving to Vermont! Mariah did eventually get her driver's license this past summer. And at the age of nineteen, all I could say was that it was time.

I never did understand exactly what the award was that Mariah received at her high school graduation. Her adviser tells me it was like the National Honor Society without the grades, which is sort of funny. Seems analogous to getting a varsity letter for being the batboy. But I was and am proud of Mariah nonetheless. And I am glad to know that her teachers at Evergreen saw something very special in her that I knew was there all along. My work ethic seems to have rubbed off on Mariah. She held down a full-time job this summer at the Isle au Haut Boat Company and also worked weekends in the kitchen at Black Dinah Chocolatiers. She was eager to return to college, even before she knew about the car.

After reading this, if you are left with questions about Simon and me, join the club. We just can't figure it out! I have a number of close male friends of which Simon is the best. We enjoy each other's company on the golf course, on the ski slope, on the water, or just plain hanging out. We don't spend nearly as much time together as we once did. But we do stay in touch regularly. I have recently scolded myself for answering the question with "just friends." That seems to diminish friendship, as if it's not equal to or even greater than a romantic connection. I have come to know that "friends" can far surpass and fulfill like no other. And my newly acquired gal friends are the perfect example of that. The women of Isle au Haut have surely rescued from disillusionment what was once idyllic in my mind.

As for the land scam at Bungie Head, to date I haven't noticed any activity in the way of clearing the lots or other aspects of the grand scheme promising to reignite the island economy. But to give the pirates the benefit of the doubt, things do tend to move slowly here on the island. And the properties for sale did not become the epidemic I feared. The same real estate signs that popped up seemingly all at once and in response to our bad spell have not increased or been replaced by "sold," or even "under contract." So all in all we live with the status quo. I have to accept the possibility that the island community as a whole did not subscribe to my perhaps warped prediction of all-inclusive degradation. The domino effect was in my mind. And the black mark that diminished the "islandness" that was forever most coveted by me fades with every passing day as life truly goes on. I still love where I live. And I still do not deny people's observations that I am living a blessed life—more so now than ever with the enriching experience of Mariah's guardianship.

This past year has been an important one for Mariah and me. It has been tough beyond words. My sister Rhonda was diagnosed with pancreatic cancer in October and passed away eight months later following the most graceful display of courage in the face of a terminal illness. My closest friend, mentor, and first captain, Alden, died the very morning of Rhonda's memorial service. The pain of the double whammy was eased only by daily contact with friends and family, of which I have grown to realize Mariah is both.

The transformation has been remarkable. I have witnessed a sulky, confrontational teen turn into a confident, responsible, beautiful, and thoughtful young woman. Our relationship continues to grow closer and stronger. I'm not sure what the future holds any more than any mother of a nineteen-year-old does. I have not had any revelations regarding "nurture or nature," and I wonder whether Mariah believes that I am a natural born mother or that she trained me. I don't suppose it matters. I couldn't love Mariah any more if she were my own flesh and blood. Yup. We are still "us." And we are great!

Alas, Mariah is not my daughter's real name. In an attempt to protect her privacy, I have changed her name, the name of her high school, and the college she is attending. Of course all those close to the situation will know Mariah's real identity—and they are all the people who continue to love and support us. My hope is that the people in the know will read this book as a bit of a love letter and a thank-you to them from me. My daughter is all in favor of my writing our story. In fact, her hope is that this book will inspire or give strength to some other young victim to break out of the cycle of abuse.

Acknowledgments

For all my talk of being independent and self-reliant, the writing of this book has been quite a revelation. And acknowledgments seem to be the place to, well, acknowledge the help and support necessary for the successful relationship between mother and daughter, and written documentation thereof.

First and foremost, thanks to my family and friends for ongoing support of my work, both seagoing and landlocked. The island community of which I write endearingly never ceases to amaze in its resilience and strength. We may be small in individual numbers, but as a cohesive unit, we speak volumes. Thanks for chiming in when it would have been so much easier and comfortable to remain silent. The good and decent folks of Isle au Haut recognized something amiss, acted quickly, and by doing so saved a life.

My immediate family is the perfect example of the "good" in my course made. The passing of my sister, Rhonda, left a huge void. But her kindness and advice on parenting a teenage girl linger. Mom and Dad, your undying loyalty, compassion, and support of all I do in the face of better judgment command my ship unconditionally. Bif is my rock, and Ben is hers. Chuck is my alter ego, and Jen his. Aubrey and Addison still split the apple of my eye. But Mariah is mine. Not of flesh and blood, but of real visceral experience. And that, it seems, is just as worthy as familial kinship.

This was a particularly tough writing assignment. And I owe so much to so many for help and guidance in its completion. Thanks to the usual suspects. To name a few; Wendy Wolf, Wil Schwalbe, and Stuart Krichevsky—editors and literary agent. Huge thanks to the entire support team surrounding publishers and agent who do all the behind-the-scenes magic that makes my work appear seamless.

Lastly, thanks to my daughter for being just that.